CRIME

Crime films have, since the earliest days of cinema, been popular with audiences, industry and critics alike and encompassed a diverse range of subjects, styles and themes. The genre provides a range of pleasures for the spectator, from taking on the role of the detective in the pursuit of clues in the 'whodunit', to the more illicit thrills of identification with an anti-hero. In the many incarnations of the crime film such as the gangster, film noir, political and detective thrillers, the genre explores the anxieties of different historical moments.

Sarah Casey Benyahia provides an overview of the development of the crime film and examines the key theories and ideas involved in the study of the genre. These include: the investigative structure and narration of the crime film, the aesthetics of violence and issues of representation and ideology. These areas are explored through contemporary and classic Hollywood and European cinema with case studies on the history of the genre, the role of the detective, the 'family crime' film and the conspiracy thriller.

Crime provides a broad framework to the study of the genre through the introduction of narrative, genre and audience theories as well as detailed analysis of specific films.

Films discussed include: *Scarface* (1932) *Mildred Pierce* (1945) *Dirty Harry* (1971) *The Parallax View* (1974) *Reservoir Dogs* (1992) *Mystic River* (2002) *Hidden* (2005) *Gone Baby Gone* (2007) *Zodiac* (2007) The Millennium Trilogy (2009) and *The Secret in Their Eyes* (2010).

Sarah Casey Benyahia is Head of Film Studies at Colchester Sixth Form College, UK. She is the author of *Teaching Contemporary British Cinema* (2005) and co-author of *AS and A2 Film Studies: The Essential Introduction* (Routledge, 2008 and 2009).

Routledge Film Guidebooks

The Routledge Film Guidebooks offer a clear introduction to and overview of the work of key filmmakers, movements or genres. Each guidebook contains an introduction, including a brief history; defining characteristics and major films; a chronology; key debates surrounding the filmmaker, movement or genre; and pivotal scenes, focusing on narrative structure, camera work and production quality.

Bollywood: a Guidebook to Popular Hindi Cinema
Tejaswini Ganti

James Cameron
Alexandra Keller

Jane Campion
Deb Verhoeven

Horror
Brigid Cherry

Film Noir
Justus Nieland and Jennifer Fay

Documentary
Dave Saunders

Romantic Comedy
Claire Mortimer

Westerns
John White

Crime
Sarah Casey Benyahia

Crime

SARAH CASEY BENYAHIA

Routledge
Taylor & Francis Group

LONDON AND NEW YORK

First published 2012
by Routledge
2 Park Square, Milton Park, Abingdon, Oxon OX14 4RN

Simultaneously published in the USA and Canada
by Routledge
711 Third Avenue, New York, NY 10017

Routledge is an imprint of the Taylor & Francis Group, an informa business

British Library Cataloguing in Publication Data
A catalogue record for this book is available from the British Library

Library of Congress Cataloging in Publication Data
Benyahia, Sarah Casey.
    Crime / Sarah Casey Benyahia.
    p. cm.—(Routledge film guidebooks ; 9)
    Includes bibliographical references and index.
    1. Crime films—History and criticism.
    2. Detective and mystery films—
    History and criticism. I. Title.
    PN1995.9.C66B49 2011
    791.43'6556--dc23
    2011021866

ISBN: 978–0–415–58140–0 (hbk)
ISBN: 978–0–415–58141–7 (pbk)
ISBN: 978–0–203–15588–2 (ebk)

Typeset in Joanna
by Swales & Willis Ltd, Exeter, Devon

MIX
Paper from
responsible sources
FSC
www.fsc.org FSC® C004839

Printed and bound in Great Britain by
TJ International Ltd, Padstow, Cornwall

CONTENTS

LIST OF FIGURES

ACKNOWLEDGEMENT

I would like to thank the following people for their help in the production of this book, my editor at Routledge Aileen Storry, her colleague Eileen Srebernik and my copy-editor Colin Morgan. I am very grateful to Claire Mortimer for her reading of the manuscript and insightful comments.

This book is for Farid.

1

THE DEVELOPMENT OF THE GENRE

Introduction and context

The crime film is a place of paradox and contradiction, where crime is a crisis and disruption but also expected and familiar, where it is recognised that crime doesn't pay but that its commission is inevitable; where crime is immoral, even evil, but the need to carry it out can be understood by the (law-abiding) audience. Criminals are frightening and repellent but also the most charismatic and appealing characters in the story. This ambiguity in subject and audience response may be one reason for the genre's appeal but also helps to explain why the definition of the 'crime film' has proven so difficult. The problem of definition is a familiar aspect of genre theory, but the crime film – without the 'strong' features of other genres – is particularly hard to pin down.

WHY DOES A DEFINITION MATTER?

Academics have disagreed over the definition of the crime genre, with studies in the area beginning with a discussion of what is and what isn't included, for example Clarens (1980) excludes the thriller while

Warshow (1962) and Shadoian (1977) define it as synonymous with the gangster genre. Many influential works have focused on a sub-set or cycle: film noir, the suspense thriller, Hitchcock's thrillers, etc. The crime genre is examined as a series of categories rather than a broad genre, or even as if it doesn't exist at all:

> The American crime film does not belong to any genre. It is more correctly classified simply as a drama. Instead, it embodies many genres. The crime drama extends from such wide areas as the detective genre, to the gangster genre, to the 'old dark house' genre. However, many crime films, such as Fritz Lang's classic *The Woman in the Window* (1944), or Billy Wilder's equally famous *Double Indemnity*, released the same year, cannot be pigeonholed into any specific genre – they simply remain dramas, in the best general sense of the term.
>
> (Langman, 1995: xviii)

In his essay 'Contemporary Crime and The Detective Film', Neale (1999a) identifies three principle genres in crime as a whole: the gangster film, detective film and suspense film. These categories can be defined by the differing focus and emphasis on key characters of the genre – the criminal, the victim and the agent of law and order (often, but not always, a detective). The choice of perspective or point of view across these figures would define whether the film was a detective film (emphasis on investigation and justice), a gangster film (focus on criminal), or a thriller (audience experience the fear and suspense of the victim).

Thompson (2007: 3) contends that the wide grouping of the crime genre can be defined as a conceptual category, starting with the question 'what do we mean by crime?' and answering with reference to the crime film's representational link to a time and place: crime as a 'social and political' act.

Bordwell (1989: 148) argues that it is a feature of genre production, that it is impossible to categorise films with complete certainty: 'The identification is transitory and heuristic, like that of nearly all the categories we draw on in everyday life. Genres, and genre, function as open-ended and corrigible schemata'. It is in this area of transition and corrigibility that the debate over definition takes place – and why it matters.

Genre theory is not just concerned with creating a taxonomy of films by iconography and conventions, but in providing a context for the understanding of the meaning of that film. The genre is the background against which the film is read – it informs our comprehension of the workings of the film. This ranges from the level of audience expectation – if it's a musical then it's logical that characters break into a song and dance with full orchestra backing – to interpretation. To watch a film in the context of a 'drama' will construct a different response than that of the context of 'crime'. Watching *Double Indemnity* (Billy Wilder, 1944) as a drama rather than a crime film will give prominence to emotional relationships over the negotiation of the relationship between criminal and society. If a thriller is not a crime film then it becomes purely about individual psychology. In this approach the importance of the question 'what is a crime film?' is shifted to 'what genres or genre constitute an effective and pertinent context for the reading of this film?' (Ryall, 1998: 336) This is particulary useful in contemporary Hollywood genre production: *No Country for Old Men* (Ethan and Joel Coen, 2007), for example, has been defined as a crime film, Western, road movie, comedy or hybrid, each categorisation changing the meaning of the film.

This introduction provides an overview of the different critical accounts used to categorise and define the crime genre within the wider framework of genre theory. Table 1.1 provides a brief overview of some of the key categories, periods and cycles of the crime genre.

These approaches are examined in the context that the most useful understanding of what a crime film is comes from its function as a negotiation of the borders between criminal and non-criminal behaviour (Leitch, 2002). The approaches discussed define the genre from historical, institutional and academic perspectives – showing

Table I.I Overview of key crime film cycles and categories

Gangster film

Characterised by the rise and fall of a 'tragic' hero in the context of organised crime. The crime family is a hierarchical structure governed by strict codes of honour and loyalty, which are always broken.

The Public Enemy, Scarface (and remake), Little Caesar, The Godfather (and sequels), Once Upon a Time in America, Goodfellas, Get Carter, Pulp Fiction, Snatch, Sexy Beast.

Film noir

A cycle of films made in Hollywood in the 1940s and early 1950s which were retrospectively named by French critics. The films encompass a range of plot lines but are distinguished by a chiaroscuro visual style which represents the typical mood of paranoia and distrust in the cycle.

Double Indemnity, Mildred Pierce, The Postman Always Rings Twice, Force of Evil, The Big Sleep, Out of the Past, Detour, Kiss Me Deadly.

Detective film

Often a hybrid form with other areas of the crime film such as, film noir, police procedural and thriller, the detective may be professional or amateur. The focus of the detective film is the process of the investigation, the solving of clues and the resolution (or otherwise) of the enigma.

The Thin Man, The Maltese Falcon, Zodiac, Seven, The Silence of the Lambs, The Secret in Their Eyes, The Lincoln Lawyer, Gone Baby Gone, Police, Adjective, Z, The Da Vinci Code, Shutter Island.

Thriller

The thriller includes a wide range of subject matter and characters but can be defined through the effect of suspense created by the relationship between detective or victim and criminal. Suspense is constructed through the emphasis on the victim and the suffering they experience. (See Derry (1988) for discussion of the different categories of thriller.)

Coma, Copycat, The Game, Hidden, Inception, Missing, North by Northwest, Rear Window, Disturbia.

Political crime film

Originally associated with American cinema of the 1970s, the political crime film – or conspiracy film – deals with the investigation of a cover up by governments or corporations. The films are characterised by a mood of paranoia often linked to downbeat endings.

Klute, The Parallax View, The Conversation, Chinatown, Three Days of the Condor, All the President's Men, Enemy of the State, Arlington Road, Michael Clayton, The Ides of March.

Vigilante film

In its pure form, the vigilante film focuses on the illegal actions of a private individual who, having been the victim of crime, enacts revenge and retribution on the criminals. This narrative of retribution is also found in the detective film with the character of the maverick cop.

Dirty Harry, The Enforcer, Magnum Force, Death Wish (and sequels), Walking Tall, Old Boy, The Brave One.

how the intersection of these three areas has affected the production and reception of crime films.

TAKING A GENRE APPROACH

Genre theory – with authorship – is one of the dominant approaches in Film Studies. It was part of the foundation of Film Studies as an institutionalised, academic subject with its own rationale and theoretical framework. Early writing on genre films (in the 1920s for example) tended to be an attack on the repetition and standardisation of Hollywood film making. This style of genre production was seen as inferior to the European art cinema tradition (see Rotha, 1930/1967), setting up the European/Art, Hollywood/Commerce opposition which is still recognisable, if more blurred, today. In this context, European cinema was the home of the auteur while Hollywood relied on genre, with all the distinctions between originality and predictability which that implied.

The implications of a genre approach can be understood in the context of an attack on authorship. Auteur theory attempted to apply the high-art concepts of individuality and authenticity to the popular and industrialised culture of film; genre theory of the 1950s and 1960s recognised that formula and repetition were central to Hollywood film production and to its appeal. Auteur theory claimed artistic status for popular film by forcing it into a model which dated back to the renaissance; genre theory was an attempt to address the value of popular cinema and acknowledge the role of the audience. Although it developed out of dissatisfaction with the auteur theory, early genre theory was still reliant on authorship as a way of explaining a genre's evolution (Ford and the Western; Fuller, Ray and Lang and the crime film) or as a way of placing auteurs within an institutional context. The later more radical rejection of auteur theory raised influential points about the relationship between film and reality, arguing that genres were signifying systems with their own rules and not just a reflection of reality, which culminated in later work on genre and ideology.

The first writings which recast the hierarchy of authorship and genre focused on clearly defined genres which seemed to have a direct relationship to American history such as the Western and the gangster genre (see Buscombe, 1970; Alloway, 1971). This approach read genres as myths with their conventional iconography and themes part of a ritual played out between production and reception. Within this context they are interpreted as a form of mimesis; reflecting the concerns of contemporary society in an attempt to explain the world. This explanation of the function of genre across contexts has been challenged effectively by Neale (1990), who argues that the 'mental condition of a nation cannot be read from consumer choice at box office'. Gledhill (2000) suggests that the key question in genre theory is to problematise the relationship between the film and the social, and look at the different ways in which films and the social interact. To achieve this she argues that there must be a rethinking of genre as an industrial mechanism, an aesthetic practice and as an arena of cultural-critical discourse.

DEFINING THROUGH ICONOGRAPHY

Analyzing the function of a genre is dependent on the categorisation of what constitutes the genre. In defining the crime genre this problem was apparent in the variety of terms used to describe the same films as well as the debate over genre, sub-genre, cycles, styles, etc. For example, is *The Maltese Falcon* (Huston, 1941) a film noir, detective film, crime film or thriller? The range of approaches used to define and categorise the gangster genre illustrate the strengths and limitations of genre theory; the following section discusses some of the influential entries in this area.

Colin McArthur's *Underworld USA* (1972) was the first sustained attempt to identify an iconography which would objectively define the genre, demonstrating the links between the gangster film of the 1930s and the thrillers of the 1940s and 1950s. *Underworld USA*, though, is also an attempt to integrate authorship and genre theory: the iconography of the gangster genre is used as a control to identify the individual characteristics of auteurs working in the genre. McArthur's aim was to demonstrate how the constraints of working within a mass-produced genre in the context of the studio system was not antagonistic to the creation of art:

> That the supposed constraints on the artist working within a commercial/industrial structure such as Hollywood may be better described as disciplines. The necessity of working within narrative and genre, with prescribed stars, a strong producer's hand and forceful collaborators, may lead not to a diminution but to an intensification of the artefact's force and range through the ironing out of its purely coterie elements. The argument could be extended to suggest that the necessity of working within fixed budgets and shooting schedules has decisively shaped the style and therefore the meaning of certain artists.
>
> (McArthur, 1972: 150)

In the context of genre definitions the introductory chapters in particular provided a definition of the gangster film which has remained influential. Ryall (1979) summarised McArthur's iconographic elements as belonging to one of three categories: the physical presence and characteristics of the actors and the characters they play; the urban milieu of the films; and the technology used by the gangster (for example, guns and cars).

McArthur argues that the gangster genre in its classic phase – the period when the all the recognisable elements of the genre are in place – lasted only two years before going into a decline and reappearing at the end of the decade. For example, by 1930 *Little Caesar* (Mervyn Leroy, 1930) includes all the iconography expected from the gangster film (guns, automobiles, telephones, the city, recognisable stars) along with the thematic concerns: the rise and fall of the gangster. McArthur's iconographic taxonomy of the classic gangster film is divided into three phases.

The first phase (1930–1934) includes films such as *Little Caesar, Public Enemy* (William Wellman, 1931) and *Scarface* (Howard Hawks, 1932). Many of the defining characteristics of this phase are to do with the central character of the gangster who is 'born not made', violent and vulgar, charismatic and tragic. All the central characters of the first phase come from immigrant Catholic backgrounds. The ethnicity of the gangster of the classic phase follows the 'ladder model' of immigration with new immigrants taking the lowest place on the ladder; gangsters are from Irish then Italian backgrounds, reflecting the patterns of immigration in the 1920s and 1930s. This theme continued through reference to Cuban gangsters – *Scarface* (Brian De Palma, 1983) – and African American gangsters – *Boys n the Hood* (John Singleton, 1991), *Dead Presidents* (Albert and Allen Hughes, 1995), *Menace II Society* (Albert and Allen Hughes, 1993) – representing those groups' immigrant and outsider experience.

This classic phase concentrates on the violence of the gangster's work and it becomes a convention of the genre that they will die in a similarly violent and often public manner. Despite the fact that the

Figure 1.1 'Do it first, do it yourself and keep on doing it'. The philosophy of the gangster is expressed by Tony Camonte (Paul Muni) in the original *Scarface*

Figure 1.2 'You look like a gangster'. The glamour of the gangster persona demonstrated by Jimmy Cagney in *The Public Enemy*

gangster is always punished, his death is shown as important, sometimes even tragic or heroic. Scorsese (1995) describes the death of Eddie Bartlett (James Cagney) at the end of *The Roaring Twenties* (Raoul Walsh, 1939) as reminiscent of a pieta. The ambiguous representation of the gangster caused the genre to be at the centre of a censorship battle. This was initially countered by producers through placing a justificatory prologue at the beginning of the films such as this from *Scarface* (1932):

> This picture is an indictment of gang rule in America and of the callous indifference of the government to this constantly increasing menace to our safety and liberty.
>
> Every incident in this picture is the reproduction of an actual occurrence, and the purpose of this picture is to demand of the government what are you going to do about it?
>
> The government is your government. What are you going to do about it?

Beyond his violent acts, the criminality of the gangster is symbolised in aspects of his lifestyle and behaviour, where he is shown to commit the crime of bad taste. The gangster is 'vulgar' in his conspicuous consumption of clothes, jewellery, homes and glamorous women, and in his garrulousness (this is in marked contrast to later gangsters such as Michael Corleone in *The Godfather* who is reserved and analytical). The gangster's 'compulsive drive for success' is too visible in a society where success is disguised as natural and deserving.

One of the pleasurable expectations of the genre for the audience is the transformation scene when the gangster tries on their new clothes, when they take on the persona of the gangster. This is the narrative signal that the gangster has arrived, but it is also the beginning of their decline. In *Public Enemy*, this is signified when Tom Powers (James Cagney) and Matt Doyle (Edward Woods) are fitted for new, custom-made suits. The film is careful to undercut any paradoxical connotations of feminine vanity by having the gangsters behave aggressively and homophobically to the tailor. Their overreaction to the situation is also an indication of their ignorance of the conventions of the world in which they now exist but can't belong. In *Goodfellas* (Martin Scorsese, 1991) the young Henry Hill appears on the doorstep to proudly show his mother his new outfit of double breasted suit, spats. 'You look like a gangster,' she responds, slamming the door in his face. Clothes become a symbol for the audience of the moral decline and self-delusion of the gangster. In a scene reminiscent of Tony Camonte's (*Scarface*, 1932) pride in the number of shirts he owns, a tracking shot in *Goodfellas* observes the number of suits in Henry's wardrobe while his wife Karen explains in a voiceover that her husband committed crimes to 'provide the little extras'.

During the first phase of the genre the gangster's sexuality is used to indicate character and their sexual relations are shown to be 'abnormal'. McArthur points to *Little Caeser* and *Scarface*, where the gangsters are linked with homosexuality and incestuous desires. The gangster's relationship with his mother is explored from the beginning of the genre, drawing on Italian cultural stereotypes and Freudian analysis of the damaged man unable to grow up. (A recent incarnation has been *The Sopranos* (HBO, 1999–2007), where the tortured relationship between the central character and his mother was the inspiration for the series.) While definitions of sexual norms may have changed, sex and sexuality is still used to indicate character later in the gangster genre: Sonny Corleone in *The Godfather* (Francis Ford Coppola, 1972) can never take up his position as head of the family because of his uncontrollable sexual appetite. The audience is introduced to him as he has illicit sex with one of the bridesmaids at his sister's wedding when he should be helping his father conduct business. He is clearly contrasted with his younger brother Michael who displays little passion of any kind. This convention of the genre suggests some of the ways that the representation of women is so problematic: often absent, they are there as objects to be looked at, to signify a personality flaw, or to be victims of the gangster's misogynistic actions.

The second phase (1935–1937) identified by McArthur includes *G-Men* (William Keighly, 1935) and *Bullets or Ballots* (William Keighly, 1936). During this phase, gangster films of the style of the first phase are still being made but with the additions of the character of the 'G men' and the exploration of a social theory of crime. These films share the visual iconography of the first phase, the major difference being that the central characters are now police/FBI agents and not gangsters. This development can be read within the context of pressure from the Production Code Administration (popularly known as the 'Hays Office'). Gangster films were popular with audiences but were also controversial. The material wealth and immoral behaviour of the film gangster fed anxieties about real crime, but also raised questions about the influence of Hollywood itself. Studio self-regulation of film content had been formalised since 1922, but with falling attendances in the early 1930s studios began to introduce controversial material – sexual innuendo, violence – in order to attract audiences. The influential Catholic pressure group, the Legion of Decency, was instrumental in tightening censorship in Hollywood through the introduction of the Production Code Administration in the early 1930s. The effect of the new regime was apparent across genres, and in the gangster film the central character was replaced by the law enforcer. These moderated entries in the genre still provided many of the pleasures of the original gangster films. *Bullets or Ballots* retains the same iconography and stars; Edward G. Robinson is ostensibly a police detective but is a 'gangster' for most of the film as he works undercover to infiltrate a gang and thereby fulfils many of the conventions of the genre.

The thematic concerns of the third phase (late 1930s) are influenced by the social-conscience films of the decade – *I'm a Fugitive from a Chain Gang* (Mervyn Le Roy, 1932), *20,000 Years in Sing Sing* (Michael Curtiz, 1932) – and apparently focus on the reasons why a young man would be drawn to a criminal life (the question for young women was why they would be attracted to a gangster). Films from this phase include, *Angels with Dirty Faces* (Michael Curtiz, 1937) and

Crime School (Brian Foy, 1938). In *Angels with Dirty Faces*, Rocky (James Cagney) and Jerry (Pat O'Brien) are childhood friends. Rocky is sent to juvenile detention for a crime they both committed. The film suggests that it is this brutalising experience which makes Rocky a gangster and that he can be saved (in a religious sense of being forgiven if not rehabilitated). In these films there is also a character who chooses the right path (Jerry becomes a priest) as a parallel to the one who goes wrong, suggesting the importance of moral choice rather than a serious consideration of the social theory of crime.

The fate of the Dead End Kids (a group of street kids who Jerry tries to help at his church and who go on to appear in a series of spin-off films) is played out between the alternative role models of gangster and priest, offering a symbolic choice for the future of American society. Despite being identified as a defining theme of the third phase of the genre, social factors were also evident in the first phase. *Public Enemy* introduces Tom Powers as a mischievous boy who is corrupted by the violence of his home life (beaten by his father, a policeman) and the opportunities for criminality provided by prohibition. The realist, almost documentary style of the establishing scenes of *Public Enemy* reinforces this link to the social context. The gangster is made not born.

DEFINING THROUGH AN IDEOLOGICAL APPROACH

The assumption that the gangster film has a direct relationship to the 'real world' is challenged in ideological analyses of the genre. In his essay 'The Gangster as Tragic Hero' (2002a [1948]), an ideological and aesthetic analysis of the genre, Robert Warshow argues that the question of whether the gangster genre explores the social context in seeking to understand criminal behaviour is irrelevant: 'we are not permitted to ask whether at some point he could have chosen to be something else than what he is' (2002a [1948]: 101). The gangster exists in the imagination and the gangster film is a work of art; the similarity to the everyday lived experience of the audience, the realism or otherwise of its depiction of organised crime, is to miss the point of the function of the genre. The gangster does not exist except as a tragic hero, an unexpected symbol of the paradox of American life: that to attempt to succeed is to fail. Warshow argues that the distinguishing characteristic of the genre is its dissonance, a refusal to conform to the 'euphoria spread over our culture like the broad smile of a happy idiot' (2002a [1948]: 98). In contrast, the gangster genre is 'an astonishingly complete presentation of the modern sense of tragedy' (2002a [1948]: 99).

The argument that popular culture can express the same themes as high art is made explicitly. Just as the Elizabethan Revenge Tragedy developed detailed conventions, the 'fixed dramatic patterns and rigidity of conventions' of the gangster genre 'is not opposed to the requirements of art' (2002a [1948]: 99). The gangster is a tragic character because he embodies a contradiction, the flaw which will lead to his death. This paradox is played out in the rise-and-fall narrative which is the drive to succeed; yet the striving for power is to separate oneself from the world. Warshow argues that all attempts at success are signs of aggression, but the drive for individualism means vulnerability and isolation: 'The gangster's whole life is an effort to assert himself as an individual, to draw himself out of the crowd, and he always dies because he is an individual; the final bullet thrusts him back, makes him, after all, a failure' (2002a [1948]: 103). The gangster as tragic hero has an ideological function, it reconciles the inherent contradiction of existence within capitalism, that we are doomed because we must succeed: 'This is our intolerable dilemma; that failure is a kind of death and success is evil and dangerous, is – ultimately – impossible. . . . The dilemma is resolved because it is his death, not ours' (2002a [1948]: 103).

At the end of the 1930s there is a radical development of the genre with *The Maltese Falcon* which both continues some of the traditions of the previous decade and breaks with the occupations of that period. The iconography remains recognisable and the actors are the figures familiar from the gangster films of the classic phase, but the tone has changed and it is this, McArthur (1972) argues, which distinguishes the gangster from the thriller. In *The Maltese Falcon* there is a 'sense of human isolation and awareness of evil' which sets it apart from the gangster film and signals the advent of film noir with its exploration of 'veiled motives and identities' which are far from the explicit manifesto of the classic gangster film. As Tony Camonte says in *Scarface*: 'Do it first, do it yourself and keep on doing it.'

In *Dreams and Dead Ends* (1977) Jack Shadoian uses the term gangster/crime film and approaches the problem of definition by asking: What does this genre do which can't be done elsewhere? This approach encompasses structural analysis, a social history of crime and the mythologising of the gangster within society and popular culture. Shadoian reads the central concern of the genre as working through a series of conflicts: 'the term versus is built into the genre'. This conflict is repeated and reinforced through structures and patterning: groups and individuals are in conflict with society; the gangster family, criminal network or isolated villain are always 'outside' of the mainstream. Conflict is societal: the gangster is not an outlaw as in the Western but a figure that violates a system of rules in society. This conflict becomes increasingly blurred as the genre develops and the lines between right and wrong in society become uncertain or corrupted.

Shadoian argues that the gangster film appeared in response to the emergence of the gangster in society but developed into metaphor and allegory (the gangster as symbol for the values of American society). The structuring conflict of the gangster/crime film, that of those on the inside and those on the outside, means that it is able to deal with any cultural concern or anxiety:

If there is a problem society is worried about or a fantasy it is ready to support, odds are it can be located in the gangster. To take what's within and place it without is to create a context for observing it with a minimum of interfering clutter.

(Shadoian, 1977: 4)

Crime films offer the law abiding audience a glimpse at a world which is strange and appealing. The pleasures available to the audience include the vicarious thrill of identifying with the outsider, the fantasy of trying on a different persona.

The definition of the crime/gangster film as any which explores the conflict between those within and those on the outside of society is very broad, highlighting some of the problems of defining the genre. Shadoian further differentiates between the gangster/crime film and other action and violence-driven genres through the identification of key themes, which while not exclusive to the gangster/crime genre are particularly suited to its structure of conflict. In this case the conflict is used to reveal the ideological construction of the American dream with the gangster as the symbol of its inherent contradiction (see Warshow, 2002a [1948]). The crime drama in general, but the figure of the gangster in particular, constantly plays out the tension between the drive for success, the fear of not having it and the consequences of achieving it.

This commentary on the destructive power of success is conceptualised in the setting of the city, 'the broadest icon of the genre'. The city is not neutral, Shadoian argues, it takes on the quality of a prison, a trap waiting for the gangster. The dual motif of the city, at once enticing and glamorous, frightening and vicious, reinforces the structuring conflict. The representation of the city in the gangster films of the 1930s is familiar from modernist discourse around the simultaneous fear and celebration of technology and mass production: the concern that mechanisation would cause destruction and alienation rather than a more efficient, happier future. (In *Scarface* (1932), Tony Camonte (Paul Muni) delights in the new mechanised weaponry: 'they've got machine guns you can carry' which will kill more people, more quickly, from a greater distance.) In films dealing with this idea in the silent period (*Metropolis* (Lang, 1927), *Sunrise* (Murnau, 1927)) the city is the location of immorality and darkness, symbolism often connoted as female. Warshow (2002a [1948]) describes the city and the gangster as inextricably linked in their status as products of the imagination rather than a real city and a real gangster. This 'dangerous and sad' place is the modern world, a place which other forms of popular culture provide an escape from through their optimism. In *Scarface* (1932), Tony Camonte's flat looks over a revolving neon advertising sign (for Cook's tours) which reads 'The World Is Yours'. This has several functions in the film – narrative and symbolic. The sign signifies the modern city as a place of opportunity and individualism; the slogan is both seductive and impossible, but the impossibility is not understood by Tony who believes in its promise. This view from Tony's flat also signifies the pinnacle of his narrative – the 'rise' of the gangster. When *Scarface* fulfills the rigid convention of the genre, that the gangster must lie dead in the street at the end of the film, the camera pans up to the revolving slogan, a visual metaphor of the defining paradox of the genre. Sixty years after *Scarface*, *La Haine* (Mattieu Kassovitz, 1995) also explores the conflict between the insiders and the outsiders of the city, as the three central characters are drawn to Paris from their home in the *banlieue* in an attempt to construct new personae. Their link to the doomed characters of the gangster genre is signified in the use of adverts with the slogan 'The World Is Yours' which appear throughout the mise en scène of the city setting.

The reading of the gangster/crime film as a metaphor for the paradox of the American dream, as expressed by Warshow (2002b [1954]), is a dominant one: 'he [the gangster] appeals to that side of all of us that refuses to believe in the "normal" possibilities of happiness and achievement; the gangster is the "no" to that great American "yes" which is stamped so big over our official culture.' The politics of the genre are ambiguous though; the gangster is an inherently conservative figure. Whether the genre is critiquing or celebrating this figure is another of the ways in which the genre plays out paradox and conflict. The gangster as businessman, as he becomes from the 1970s onwards, is clearly positioned as a right-wing pragmatist; the pursuit of money and power overrides all other concerns, even family. While the 1930s gangster existed in a context of social and economic deprivation which partly explained and excused his behavior, the later gangster/crime film seems to suggest that the tactics of the gangster are the only sane response to a weak and corrupt society – something shared with the figure of the vigilante in the revenge-cycle films of the period, for example *Death Wish* (Michael Winner, 1974), *Dirty Harry* (Don Siegel, 1971). Both gangster and vigilante films share the concern that the police are ineffective and the law is best administered by the criminal. Perhaps the strongest argument for the increasingly right-wing perspective of the genre is its nostalgia for the old country, for mother, for a time when people obeyed the rules.

DEFINING THROUGH FORM AND AESTHETIC EFFECT

To define a genre by its intended effect and its form (horror, comedy, thrills, etc.) does have many problems. Is the intended effect the same as the actual experience? Does that affect a definition? If form is a defining characteristic, then how to distinguish between the use of stock characters and classic narrative used by most mainstream Hollywood genres? In the crime genre a lot of work has focused on these areas of narrative structure and audience positioning, arguing that there is something specific about their workings in this genre which isn't found elsewhere. It is the case, though, that most of this work has been carried out on crime films which feature the figure of the detective and are structured around an investigation. Analysis of the detective film category encompasses a wide range of films and reveals more of the contradictions in defining the genre. It can be stated that the detective film's narrative follows an investigation and that there is a protagonist that functions as a detective. It is also the case that the detective film may focus on exploring the detective rather than the enigma of the investigation; if the focus is on the investigation then it may not be carried out by a professional detective. The detective is nearly always a man, though, which has led to readings of the detective film as not just an investigation into a crime but an investigation into masculinity itself. (When a female detective does appear in crime films then the discussion is always about gender.) Gates (2004) uses the figure of the actual or surrogate detective as a framework for creating sub-genres of the detective film. Through this it is argued that the genre follows a traditional trajectory, evolving from a classical model, developing through stages of hybridity, before returning to an approximation of the purity of the early form. Thus we have the classical detective, transitional detective (associated with Hollywood in the 1930s – 'hard boiled' but without the cynicism of the later detective of film noir), the noir detective, police and procedure, vigilante cop, cop as action hero, and the criminalist, whose cerebral approach is closer to the early detectives.

These detective categories are roughly chronological and seem to mirror perceived changes in society and culture. The detective types develop from the upper-class gentleman sleuth to the blue-collar average guy, from detection as hobby to police work as a professional career. The vigilante (and maverick) cop of the 1960s and 1970s symbolises the distrust of the police as another example of an institutionally corrupt organisation (*Serpico* (Sidney Lumet, 1973), *The Prince of the City* (Sidney Lumet, 1981)) and an increasingly violent, immoral society (*Coogan's Bluff*, *Dirty Harry*). Towards the end of the twentieth century the genre is characterised by the explicit mixing of the detective and action film, leading to a new figure, 'the cop as action hero', which draws on the hyper-masculinity of Hollywood action heroes (*Lethal Weapon* (Richard Donner, 1987), *48 Hours* (Walter Hill, 1982)). The concept of enigma and investigation was sidelined for the emphasis on spectacle, action and the hero's body. The emergence of the 'criminalist' or thinking hero, highly trained, scientific and objective, can be read in opposition to the action detective, with the formal structure of the investigation becoming central (*Seven*, *The Silence of the Lambs*, *The Da Vinci Code*). This category also offers a more contemporary representation of society with detectives who are female, older and from a range of ethnic backgrounds.

The argument that the detective figure provides a reflection of changes in society is encountered repeatedly in writing about detective literature as well as films. The emergence of the detective as a cultural phenomenon is linked to the introduction of the professional detective in the mid-nineteenth century and the wider context of an increasingly secular society which was concerned with scientific and rational explanations for events. The character of the detective in literature and the development of the crime novel provide some interesting connections and context for the genre in film. As with the film genre, the categorisation of fictional writing about crime are complicated: 'the generic terms thriller and mystery are now too blurred for descriptive use' (Drabble, 1985: 269); instead, categories are defined around narrative structure and audience positioning. The detective story relies on the process of 'investigation, observation and deduction' by a private or professional detective to resolve the mystery and reveal the identity of the criminal. The crime novel, in contrast, reveals the identity of the criminal from the start: the focus becomes the observation of psychological development and whether his attempts to escape justice will be successful. The 'hidden secret' (or sensation) novel is closest to the suspense thriller in film, focusing on a crime which is slowly revealed to the characters and reader without explicit deduction.

The first detective stories are generally considered to be Edgar Allan Poe's Dupin series, which began with 'The Murders in the Rue Morgue' (1841). The first English detective story was later, Wilkie Collin's *The Moonstone* (1868) but the popularity of detection was confirmed with the international success of the character of Sherlock Holmes, whose seemingly superhuman feats of deduction celebrated the superiority of rational thought over superstition and religion. The appeal of the detective is explained, once again, as performing the function of myth, in explaining the inexplicable: 'Amid the uncertainties of the mid-19th century, a detective offered science, conviction, stories that could organise chaos. He turned brutal crimes – the vestiges of the beast in man – into intellectual puzzles' (Summerscale, 2008).

Several characteristics that are recognisable in the contemporary film detective are apparent in the golden age of the classic literary detective: they are obsessive and determined, with empty or tragic personal lives; their work is their life; and because of this they have the moral authority to administer punishment in a secular age. Also noticeable is how quickly the representation of the detective darkens and becomes ambiguous: the detective is quickly seen as a threat, someone who will break down the protection of birth and class – even violating the home – to reveal the truth.

The narrative organisation of the detective film is central to the genre's aim to create curiosity about past events (what happened?), suspense (what will happen in the future?) and the surprise of the unexpected. This aim is achieved through the interplay of the suppression of knowledge and its revelation, and is developed through various tactics of narration: the relationship of fabula to syuzhet, omniscient and restricted, retardation. Besides formalist approaches to narrative analysis, psychoanalytic approaches have been used to discuss the pleasure provided by detective films. The desire to 'know' and simultaneously the wish to delay this knowledge, to draw out the pleasurable expectation experienced in watching detective films, has been interpreted as relating to fantasies of the 'primal scene'. The desire to reveal the ultimate source of knowledge is also a fantasy which places the subject as voyeur. These digressions and delaying tactics – the retardation – of the detective narrative are a central convention of the genre. It commonly uses plot twists and red herrings, unmarked ellipsis which hide information from the spectator, subplots and parallel investigations, romantic developments which pause the narrative, and characters who appear to help but who are really there to delay the action (Dr Watson is Sherlock Holmes's 'blocking character' – see Porter, 1981).

In his work on narrative and the poetics of film, Bordwell (2007) develops the Russian formalist concepts of fabula and syuzhet to demonstrate how the crime film is distinguished by a specific narrative organisation. The fabula is all the events of the story or all the events which are known, 'the story's state of affairs'; the syuzhet refers to the selection and arrangement of the fabula into the narrative. The flashback is an example of how the syuzhet reorganises the chronological fabula. Bordwell's narrative analysis of these concepts in the crime film separates the fabula – the story of the crime, the story of the investigation – and the syuzhet – the manipulation of the story of the crime and the investigation. This is the aim and appeal of the detective film: the restriction and revelation of knowledge constructs an emotional response for the spectator. It could be argued that the problem of defining the detective film through an analysis of narrative construction is that all genres rely on the withholding and revelation of information for the emotional response of the audience. The romantic comedy uses restricted narration to withhold the true nature of one of the characters in order to create a more emotional revelation and resolution; the sci-fi film restricts audience knowledge to that of the hero's as he/she attempts to open the air lock, etc. Other criticisms have accused this analysis of turning all films into 'detective' films: 'in an important sense every narrative does depend on uncertainties, the most basic concerning what will happen next' (Bordwell, 2007: 101). The universality of this structure has a specific purpose in the crime film: to explore the shifting lines of criminality and innocence, the definition of outsiders and insiders within society (not outside of it as in the Western, or within an individual psychology as in the horror film), and how this line is patrolled.

IS IT A CRIME FILM? THE THRILLER

The argument that there is no need to categorise the crime genre by sub-set has been most repeatedly challenged by reference to the gangster genre and the thriller. While the separateness of the gangster film has been based on iconography, the definition of the thriller as different from the crime film is based on the construction of suspense, the different role of criminal and victim, and specifically their symbolic relationship to their time and place (Smith, 1995). A dominant approach to defining the thriller is through the aesthetic effect of suspense in contrast to the surprise created by the relationship between detective and criminal. Suspense is constructed through the emphasis on the victim and the suffering they experience. The victim often has knowledge of how they are being victimised and this knowledge is shared with the audience. Derry (1988: 31–54) emphasises the importance of curiosity over surprise in the thriller – the audience must have an expectation about what will happen next rather than the effect of shock and surprise. Suspense is a structural device which functions by providing the audience with all the relevant information and constructing a range of possible expectations. This curiosity is focused on '(how) will the protagonist survive?' and is therefore linked to the close alignment between audience and victim in the thriller. The structural device of suspense is then reinforced through narrative themes of opposition and duality (most clearly in the similarities and differences between the victim and the villain) and in stylistic devices such as cross-cutting, which manipulates the audience identification and alignment with character. The victim is often an 'everyman' who does not have the professional training to deal with the situation they find themselves in. This central situation is discussed in the context of philobats (lovers of thrills) and ocnophobes (haters of thrills); the plot of the thriller takes the ocnophobe protagonist and places them in deadly but thrilling situations (for example, *North by Northwest*, *The Fugitive*, *Arlington Road*, *Shadow of a Doubt*, etc.).

In *Crime Movies*, Clarens (1980) states that thrillers are a 'close relative' of the crime film rather than part of the same genre and outlines the differences between a thriller and a crime film. He concludes that thrillers are too personal and individual to have the representational function of the crime film. The characters in a thriller are less emblematic, the criminal viewpoint is more esoteric than in the crime genre: the motive of gangsters, bank robbers and hustlers are far more explicit and pragmatic. For Clarens the relationship between the characters and society is tenuous in the thriller: 'society is not directly involved and therefore absolved from responsibility' (1980: 13), thus apparently removing one of the defining features of the crime film. The definition of crime films as those which have a direct, representational relationship to the society which produced them is evident in the thematic organisation of chapters in *Crime Movies*, which reference US political and social contexts: 'The First Crusade' (increased power of the FBI in the 1930s and 1940s), 'New Deal for the Gangster' and 'All Quiet the Home Front' (post-war propaganda). In this definition of the thriller, violence exists only in the private sphere and therefore the detective's role can be usurped at any time by the victim or even the criminal: the heroes of thrillers only represent themselves; the heroes of crime films 'represent the criminal, the law and society' (Clarens, 1980: 13). Clarens's defintition of the crime genre as the 'expression of America's changing attitude toward crime. Crime films work in terms of transgression and retribution' (ibid.) is actually fairly narrow, in this context a film is only capable of doing this through specific reference to the official representatives of justice – police, lawyers, FBI, judges, etc., fighting clearly defined criminals with understandable motives. In counter to this, Leitch (2002: 12) argues that 'thrillers are crime films that focus on the victims of crimes, or of the criminal justice system', thereby still performing the function of discussing the relationship between criminal, victim and society.

FORMALIST APPROACH TO THE CRIME FILM: THE MILLENNIUM TRILOGY

The different workings of the crime film narrative can be analysed within the individual entries in 'The Millennium Trilogy' (*The Girl with the Dragon Tattoo, The Girl Who Played with Fire, The Girl Who Kicked the Hornet's Nest*) and across the three films. The analysis also demonstrates the importance to interpretation of reading the trilogy as crime films rather than separate categories of drama, thriller, detective story, etc. – the crime film encompasses all of these elements.

The overarching narrative construction of the trilogy aims, at different points, to create curiosity, suspense and surprise for the viewer through the manipulation of the fabula and the changing identificatory position of the audience. This shifts from identification with the first 'detective', Michael Blomkvist, an anti-establishment investigative journalist, to the second, Lisbeth Salander, an alienated figure with a violent past who works as a hacker (or 'cracker'). The trilogy develops from the form of the classical detective story, the 'whodunit', with the familiar figure of the crusading journalist, to a suspense thriller whose purpose is to provide audience pleasure in the vindication of Salander, after she has been attacked and framed by the state. The fabula does contain storylines which can be read as an explicit attack on Swedish hypocrisy and corruption (these include familiar crime film plots which reveal old men as secret Nazis who are symbolic of the country's hidden past; heads of corporations prepared to go to any length to protect a profit; government knowledge and complicity in the work of a secret police force which can no longer be controlled, etc.) but the narrative focus is more on the contemporary uncertainty about the shifting relationship between the power of the state and the individual in the era of new technology. In the context of the crime film, the narrative structure of the Millennium Trilogy functions as a discourse about the policing of society in the virtual world; here the borders between detective and criminal, legal behavior and criminality are entering new territory. The two central characters represent the different sides of this line: the real versus the virtual world, community versus isolation, public versus private good. The conflict at the core of this crime film is a response to the new world: what role is there for traditional concepts of morality and ethics in an ungoverned space. As the gangster films of the 1930s were read as anxieties about the future of cities in a time of rapid change, the Millennium Trilogy explores similar anxieties about cyber space. It also questions assumptions about the nature of the outsider – who is it who will be able to challenge corrupt authority? The paradox here is that the understanding of computer technology which gives Salandar power over institutions also means that she is unable to live as part of society. These ideas are found at the level of audience identification which culminates in alignment with Lisbeth Salander, the outsider.

The interplay of knowledge restricted and revealed is manipulated in many ways in the first of the Millennium Trilogy, *The Girl with the Dragon Tattoo*. The fabula covers approximately forty years; the syuzhet several weeks. Therefore the gap between the two will increase the amount of manipulation in the syuzhet. The story's 'state of affairs' includes the ostensible 'whodunit' of the film, the disappearance of a teenage girl from a remote island in the 1960s, her past family context of abuse, and relatives who are revealed to be killers. This crime is being investigated in the present by Blomkvist, who is waiting to start a prison sentence for libel against a businessman he has accused of corruption in his magazine; Blomkvist believes he has been set up. A parallel story concerns Lisbeth Salander, who as a young girl was abused by her father and in retaliation threw acid in his face and set fire to him. For this she was admitted to a psychiatric hospital

Figure 1.3 The typical mise en scène of the classical detective story in *The Girl with the Dragon Tattoo*

and has now been released on probation under the licence of a lawyer 'guardian'. Salander works for a private security firm, gaining and passing on information through hacking into computers. She is tracking Blomkvist's investigation by hacking his computer, following his progress and solving enigmas in the case before he does. In many ways the film's narrative and the figure of the 'detective' are close to the nineteenth-century literary invention and the classic whodunit – it is the story of the investigation.

The narrative organisation relies on restricted and omniscient narration which in turn manipulates audience identification. The information withheld and the questions posed in the syuzhet include: information about Salander's past; what happened to the dead/missing woman; and why Salander is 'stalking' Blomkvist. The restricted narration remains throughout the detective structure, the audience finds out information as Blomkvist and Salander do, culminating in the resolution of all the enigmas set up at the outset – apart from those about Salander's past. Throughout the film the audience is aligned with Blomkvist, given access to his personal and family life as well as an understanding of his emotional response to situations. Although the details of how he has been framed are not revealed until the end of the film, there is never any doubt for the viewer that he has been. The story and the process of identification reveals Blomkvist to be morally good, a fairly uncomplicated figure of justice fighting evil. In contrast, Salander remains distant and unknowable. The enigma of her past violence and her present criminal actions (hacking, vigilantism) are a barrier to alignment (although the audience may feel sympathy for her situation). The fabula and syuzhet of the first film are conventional of the crime film – and of mainstream narrative cinema – this changes at the level of syuzhet in the second and third films and this is indicative of a function specific to the crime film.

The syuzhet of the trilogy can be understood as developing in the following way: The Girl with the Dragon Tattoo relies on the techniques of restricted narration and retardation to create curiosity and surprise for the viewer and identification with the 'good' character. *The Girl Who Played with Fire* (Daniel Alfredson, 2009, Sweden) separates the two detective figures, giving more prominence to Salander. The plot again uses restricted narration and retardation but this time the audience is positioned with Salander, discovering the secrets of her past – who her father is, that he is alive, that she has a step-brother – as she does. In *The Girl Who Kicked the Hornet's Nest* (Daniel Alfredson, 2009, Sweden) the syuzhet has shifted from restricted to omniscient narration. All the enigmas have been revealed to the audience in the first and second films; the function of this film is to provide pleasure and satisfaction through experiencing Salander's public vindication – the fantasy of the primal scene. This shift means that Blomkvist becomes a blocking character, drawing out the pleasure of anticipation for the viewer which climaxes in a courtroom scene, another conventional motif of the crime film. Salander is victorious due to her mastery of digital technology and this is always carried out in the context of subterfuge and surveillance, unregulated by either the professional ethics of print journalism or contained by existing laws. At the final resolution of the trilogy, Blomkvist, the symbol of traditional investigative journalism which values selflessness in the pursuit of justice, is sidelined and redundant.

The manipulation of identification in response to the character of Salander is an example of what Murray Smith (1995) refers to as 'structures of sympathy'. In this analysis, forms of narration may force the audience to identify with a character through tying them together in terms of knowledge, while there may be other aspects which tell the audience that they shouldn't align themselves with a character morally. With no enigma or 'whodunnit' left to puzzle in the final instalment, the aim of the film seems to be to position Salander as a new kind of hero for the crime film, one who can police the new, virtual world to be fought over. That the audience is intended to experience pleasure in Salander's exoneration at trial is clear in the use of omniscient narration. The audience – and all the main characters – know that Salander has the evidence (in the form of a secret recording) to disprove the prosecution's claims about her character. We also all know that the evidence will be shown. There is no cliff-hanger or suspense about this situation, therefore the pleasure is entirely about the humiliation of the 'enemy' and the sharing of Salander's victory. The aftermath of the events shown on the secret film, when Salander sexually assaulted the lawyer for revenge, is not referred to. Salander's outsider status is underlined in the courtroom scene through costume: she has changed from hospital gown, then tracksuit back to her gothic style of clothes, hair and makeup, a particularly distancing and alienating style of dress for the mainstream society.

The controversy around the films (and the books from which they were adapted) centered on the representation of violence and gender. The most extreme act of violence in the trilogy belongs to the vigilante tradition in crime films linked to a reversal of gender characteristics (see also Jodie Foster in *The Brave One*). This symbolic approach to law, order and justice is reinforced in Salander's approach to the new territory of the internet. Right and wrong is yet to be determined and Salander represents an extreme individualism, alone and alienated from society with no sense of conforming to society's conventions. The sustained alignment of the audience with the character in the final instalment – at the expense of the viewer's relationship with Blomkvist – suggests an ideological allegiance to the isolation of Salander. The dissonance in the audience's relationship with her – the disruptions to a shared moral code, our well-trained expectation to align with the traditional, crusading hero – suggests that the dilemmas facing the policing of the internet are yet to be resolved.

Salander's crusade to punish her father for his violence against her has the effect of revealing the hidden workings of the Swedish government and its security services, and the corruption of national corporations and their links to Nazi history, but these are revealed by chance. Unconventionally for a hero, her quest is driven by self-obsession without any of the sense of wider moral force that agents in the crime film usually have.

The analysis of the Millennium Trilogy illustrates how the different approaches to defining the crime genre can be applied and how these create a specific interpretation. The films can be defined through iconography in the typical settings of a closed, secretive community and the corrupt and alienating city, as well as the emphasis on technology. The two detective figures conform to expectations of character types, mixing elements of the maverick, criminologist and counter-cultural detectives. The formal and aesthetic effect is typical of the crime genre: withholding and revealing information to force alignment for the audience with certain characters (and against others), providing pleasure through the manner of the hero's vindication both intellectually and physically. Ideologically the films use the central structuring opposition of the crime film – the conflict between good and evil – to examine questions of crime and punishment in contemporary society. The following chapters develop these approaches by examining other categories, themes and forms of the crime film to construct an overview of the function and appeal of this diverse genre.

2

THE APPEAL OF VIOLENCE

Violence and the crime genre are intertwined, continually controversial and appealing. Violence is part of the genre's expectations and conventions but the nature and prominence of violence changes dramatically across the range and period of crime films. The violence may be explicit and gory or it may be the threat of violence, suggested but not seen, which creates an atmosphere of anxiety. Discussions of violence in the crime film are characterised by the wider debate about the relationship between cinematic representation and the real world; mimesis or art. The response to violence in the crime film often ignores the status of film as a construction, interpreting it instead as having a direct, reflective relationship to the society which produced it, leading to intense controversy and 'moral panics'. Writing about screen violence has tended to focus on: violence as a signifier of character morality, spectator pleasure, audience effects, misogyny and representations of masculinity. The representation of violence in cinema is shaped in part by wider institutional and societal contexts which can be contradictory: regulation and censorship of film content, commercial pressures and the need to attract target audiences, social pressures about what is acceptable. While problems of definition in the crime film are evident, violence has rarely been seen as a defining feature of the genre, or as a way of distinguishing between different types of crime films.

This chapter examines the different approaches to, and contexts of, violence in crime film, considering the history of censorship, the affect and effect of violent scenes and the glamorisation of the criminal.

CENSORSHIP AND IDEOLOGY

Scenes of violence – along with sex and political messages – have been the most common reason for censorship of films. The censorship and regulation of film production has always been both ideological and pragmatic, whether motivated by beliefs about the effect of films on parts of the audience or as a way of protecting business interests (Hollywood studios introduced the Production Code Administration, a form of self-regulation, to avoid being controlled by the US government, with which they were threatened in the 1920s). The censorship of violence in the crime film, but also in related genres such as the horror and the Western, is the result of responses to moral panics about the ideological messages supposedly promoted by the function of violence in the films. In the crime film this has been particularly provoked by audience alignment with a charismatic anti-hero.

As the dominant global film institution, the Production Code Administration – the censorship system of Hollywood – has been the most influential and the one most familiar to audiences. Will Hays was appointed as president of the MPPDA (Motion Picture Producers and Distributors of America) in 1922 by the industry to improve the public image of Hollywood (after scandals involving famous film stars such as Mary Pickford and Fatty Arbuckle) and to protect Hollywood's economic interests. On his appointment, Hays launched a campaign for films to be protected under the First Amendment – freedom of speech – arguing that film was an art-form rather than a business and should therefore have protection under that amendment. This campaign was a political strategy with no expectation of success: the aim was to shift the debate from the attacks on Hollywood and to question the seeming consensus that Hollywood film was an immoral, cynical product produced only for profit. It was only in 1957 that the US Supreme Court ruled that film was covered by the First Amendment, one of the final signifiers that the Production Code was no longer relevant. The end of the Production Code, like its founding, was the result of the interconnection of ideology, business interests and changing social attitudes. Most influentially, declining audiences, due in large part to the lure of the new and (relatively) more explicit medium of TV, led to the virtual ignoring of the Production Code in an attempt to offer something different, more adult and contemporary to the audience. Films by European auteurs such as Antonioni and Rossellini, which were exhibited in US cities, dealt with sexual subject matters in a much more frank way, making Hollywood product seem dated and irrelevant. The challenges to the Code are clearly seen in films such as *Baby Doll, Lolita* and *The Pawnbroker* which ignored the prohibitions of the Production Code in the context of representations of sexuality.

The changes in representing violence were more gradual. The relaxing of rules on violent scenes led to a much more complex change in film-making than that effected by explicit sex scenes. This was apparent in the limits of what could be shown and the moral shift created by questioning established norms of right and wrong. For the viewer this would create a paradoxical position of both enjoying the violent spectacle and decrying the violent act – the foundation of much anxiety about the experiencing of violence on screen. Kolker (1988: 56–7), in his analysis of *Bonnie and Clyde* (Arthur Penn, 1968), one of the key 'end of Code' films, analyses the way that Penn's intention to generate a questioning response to violence on screen and in life ended in failure: 'Despite his effort to create a special context for the slaughter, to understand it and attempt to make the viewer consider it as well as react to it, the obvious pleasure it created was taken by film-makers as a signal that audiences wanted and would pay for more extended killings.'

The censorship of Hollywood between the 1930s and 1950s was based on a specific moral and ideological view of society, one based on Catholicism and capitalism. The strictures of the Code (as it became known in 1934) were detailed and precise with reference to the treatment of sexuality on screen but make more general commentary about representations of violence. With reference to the representation of sex, the following were prohibited: nudity, suggestive dances, discussions of sexual perversity (perversity refers to homosexuality here), miscegenation, lustful kissing and scenes of passion. In contrast, the references to crime are overarching, affecting the narrative and plot of a film:

> No picture shall be produced which will lower the moral standards of those who see it. Hence the sympathy of the audience shall never be thrown to the side of crime, wrong-doing, evil or sin. Law, natural or human, shall not be ridiculed, nor shall sympathy be created for its violation.
>
> (The Production Code 1930. http://www.screenonline.org.uk/film/id/592022/)

These prohibitions about the moral standards and audience alignment in response to film are directly related to the crime film – particularly the figure of the gangster, where the sympathy of the audience is often 'thrown to the side of crime'. In Britain there was a very similar prohibition on violent and criminal content. Public Enemy was banned in 1931 by the British Board of Film Censorship (later changed to 'Classification') due to its 'subversive depiction of crime and gangsterism' (Kochberg, 1999: 50).

The Production Code can be seen as part of the ideological construction of the classical Hollywood film, which could function as a form of propaganda; a series of representations which appeared natural but was an inherently conservative world view. Here, deference, loyalty and hard work were the key to success, love conquers all and possibilities are endless, the family is the most important unit in society and loyalty to the family doubles as a symbol of a character's patriotism. In this reading, the Production Code is a solution to the influential belief that popular culture in general and cinema in particular is a powerful medium which could directly influence the audience's feelings and actions in an instructional way. Due to this, cinema had to be carefully controlled to ensure that the correct message was conveyed. This view of cinema illustrates some of the wider debates about the role and function of cinema within society, particularly its influence on a mass audience.

MASS CULTURE THEORY

Concern about the representation of violence in the crime film can be understood in the context of a diverse theoretical debate about the effects of the, still new, medium of popular film on a mass audience.

The ideological motivation to censor and regulate films, which is associated with a right-wing analytical perspective, is mirrored in the anxieties about the effect of mass culture from a left-wing analysis. For both groups, the concerns overlap in seeing cinema as powerful and its audience as vulnerable. Pro-censorship groups are concerned that the effects may be revolutionary, criminal or anti-social. Mass culture theorists worry that it will have a much more pacifying effect, inuring the audience to the inherent inequalities of capitalism. Both positions rely on a literal analysis of Hollywood cinema, arguing that the actions on screen can have a direct influence on the audience's lives. In 'The Culture Industry: Enlightenment as Mass Deception' (2002 [1944]), Adorno and Horkheimer characterise the audience as a mass, rather than individual spectators, who will respond in a uniform and predictable way to Hollywood cinema. Hollywood genre production limits response to a prescribed reaction because the standardisation and conventional nature of genre cinema does not allow for individuated reactions or analysis: 'By craftily sanctioning the demand for rubbish it inaugurates total harmony' (Adorno, 2002 [1944]: 110). Therefore the form itself – genre – contains an ideological message of conformity and repetition. This message is then reinforced through the content, which is a form of instruction for remaining passive and unquestioning; this is illustrated through the example of animation: 'they hammer into every brain the old lesson that continuous friction, the breaking down of all individual resistance, is the condition of life in this society. Donald Duck in the cartoons and the unfortunate in real life get their thrashing so that the audience can learn to take their own punishment' (ibid.). In this view of 'masscult' the control and monitoring by a body such as the Hays Office is unnecessary as the consumer is rendered helpless in false consciousness: 'The pernicious love of the common people for the harm done to them outstrips even the cunning of the authorities. It surpasses the rigor of the Hays Office' (ibid.: 106).

'The Culture Industry' is not an attack on all forms of popular culture or even on all of the output of Hollywood. It argues instead that the Hollywood film style from the mid-1930s onwards was inextricably linked to the organisation of the Hollywood studio system on a factory model. In this context film narrative becomes another element of mass production, along with the hierarchies of labour, star contracts, production units to streamline genre production, self-censorship and domination of (world wide) film exhibition. Before this standardisation of production, Hollywood did produce work which allowed for individual spectator response and which challenged dominant ideology in a way that by the mid-1940s, Adorno is arguing, only avant garde art and high culture could. These references to more challenging forms of film tended to be to the late silent, pre-studio system era of Greta Garbo and Betty Boop rather than Micky Rooney and Donald Duck. The thesis of 'The Culture Industry' is that the individual has become a consumer in Western capitalism, producing a happy acceptance of the status quo and providing an explanation for the absence of the predicted revolution. The resistance to the culture industry could only come through the rejection of 'masscult' and the active engagement with high art, a prescription which led to accusations of elitism that Adorno directly addressed:

> Connoisseurship and expertise are proscribed as the arrogance of those who think themselves superior, whereas culture distributes its privileges

> democratically to all. Under the ideological truce between them, the con-
> formism of the consumers, like the shamelessness of the producers they
> sustain, can have a good conscience. Both content themselves with the
> reproduction of sameness.
>
> (Adorno, 2002 [1944]: 106)

The final phrase is clearly a reference to genre film-making, but also an explicit attack on Benjamin's 'The Work of Art in the Age of Mechanical Reproduction' (1992 [1936]), which provided an opposing analysis, arguing that mass culture – the art of mechanical reproduction – was a democratic form, destroying the aura associated with high art which demanded a servile and conformist response in the audience.

An important part of the mass culture critics' argument is based on concerns about the relationship between film, reality and the position of the spectator who experiences it. Their analysis was that the mass audience did not have the resources to deconstruct the illusion created on screen, accepting it as a message from nowhere, produced by no one, unable to resist the predictable 'Built-in Reaction' (MacDonald 1963: 14). This illusion was reinforced by advances in technology which worked to make film more 'real' through more closely replicating the external everyday world and using emotionally manipulative techniques such as soundtracks. The analysis and conclusions of left and right about the potential of cinema are based on the understanding that the mass audience mistakes film for reality; they cannot distinguish between representation and real life. This belief, although widely challenged in academic contexts, remains an influential 'common sense' argument in popular and political arguments about the effects of on-screen violence. Cherry (2009: 202–6) sees this argument as a condemnation of popular culture and its working-class audience, which has changed little since the mass culture critics of the 1940s. Cherry demonstrates how this argument is played out in the 'video nasties' campaign of the 1980s, when a belief that particular groups in society were vulnerable to behavioural changes as a result of watching violent films led to the banning of many horror films through the introduction of the Video Recordings Act (1984). Cherry argues that the Act was political and used film as a scapegoat for wider problems in society. In her analysis of the relationship between film violence and real-life acts of violence she points out that those films which have actually been cited in criminal cases, for example *The Matrix*, *The Basketball Diaries* and *The Fisher King*, tend to be the more mainstream films with less graphic representations of violence than those cited by pro-censorship campaigners (*Saw*, *Hotel*, *Texas Chainsaw Massacre*, etc.), demonstrating the ideological motivation of those pro-censorship groups (as well as emphasising the complexity of linking screen and real violence).

THE MEANING OF VIOLENCE: VIOLENCE AND MORALITY

The end of the Production Code in 1968 and the introduction of a ratings and classification system was met by a form of artistic self-censorship on the part of film-makers (Clarens, 1980: 293). This was demonstrated in the understanding that if violence was going to be represented more explicitly then it would need to be dramatically justified. This concept of justified or warranted violence was a continuation of the perception of film as a form of moral messaging to a mass society and has similarities with the Production Code rule of 'compensating moral values' (1934). This provision dictated that if a character – usually female – engaged in behaviour outlawed by the Code (illicit relationship, lustful behaviour, etc.) it could only be allowed if the character was shown to suffer because of it. This 'compensation' would usually take the form of self-sacrifice (giving up a lover for the good of others) or a 'natural' punishment (death from illness, the death of a relative, etc.). Despite the end of the Production Code, it was understood by film-makers that violence would have to be 'right' to be socially acceptable and therefore receive a low classification. This argument about the function of violence in film, that it is there to illustrate the 'right' side of a moral conflict, that it was acceptable when on the side of the legal authority, was soon revealed to be naive as certainties about exactly which side and what was 'right' became increasingly blurred. A related reaction to the easing of censorship was to foreground the violence in film, to make it explicit and sensuous. This approach treated violence as part of the film language in the context of film as art, rather than a mimetic representation of the workings of society. These differing institutional, social and aesthetic contexts can be traced in developments in the crime film of the 1960s.

Clarens (1980: 294) argues that violence in the Hollywood cinema of the late 1960s and 1970s becomes an 'all-purpose metaphor' for violence in society, a replacement for what might otherwise be a divisive political message. This depiction of violence could be read as either a left- or right-wing critique of American values without alienating the audience. The reading of crime films as representations of society is clear in Clarens's overview of the development of different types of crime heroes and how they embody, or are substitutions for, contemporary issues such as the Vietnam War. The absence of films about Vietnam in Hollywood until the late 1970s (The Deer Hunter, Michael Cimino, 1978; Coming Home, Hal Ashby, 1978) has been attributed to the extreme controversy and divided opinion about the war. Any film taking a pro or anti stance would risk alienating much of the total audience, so, instead, film-makers used the new violence and the new types of anti-authoritarian figures it produced as a symbol of the war. For example, Arthur Penn has discussed how Bonnie and Clyde was intended to be read as a counter-cultural statement about characters who were 'shaking things up', questioning the role of the US government at home and abroad – specifically the intervention in Vietnam. Slocum (2001) posits that the violence in American cinema of the 1960s and 1970s represents a 'golden age' of violence which was anti-establishment and counter-cultural. The special-effects driven violent cinema of the 1980s, by contrast, has no such anti-establishment meaning, or any reference beyond the act of violence itself.

The crime film, and particularly the roles of the maverick cop and vigilante killer, were developed against a backdrop of conflict and struggle in society which was crystallised in the rationale for the US invasion of Vietnam, the protests against the war and the repercussions of those protests. These included an explicit distrust of authority and the state, a questioning of whether an individual's responsibility was to the state or themselves, the justification – or otherwise – of violence. These issues were played out in the crime film, but unlike the gangster film of the 1930s it was through the character of the policeman rather than the criminal: 'a seventies paradox, the cop embodied the traumas and tensions of the decade better than the criminal' (Clarens, 1980: 298).

THE MAVERICK COP AND CHARISMATIC LEGITIMACY

The apotheosis of the maverick policeman as symbol of tensions in society is Harry Callahan, the central figure of the 'Dirty Harry' films (*Dirty Harry*, 1971, *Magnum Force*, 1973, *The Enforcer*, 1976, *Sudden Impact*, 1983), played by Clint Eastwood. Slocum (2001: 9) argues that violence functions as the representation of the 'social dynamics of power, subordination and subversion' as well as shedding a light on the meaning of masculinity. The narrative of *Dirty Harry* – and its sequels – plays out against exactly the kind of societal traumas and tensions referred to by Clarens. Like the hero of a Western, Harry doesn't fit into any established groups, neither the establishment nor the counter-culture and his rejection of both creates his position as the eternal outsider. The theme of the policeman replacing the Western hero had been dealt with explicitly in *Coogan's Bluff* (Siegel, 1968) where an Arizona policeman (also played by Clint Eastwood) is sent to New York to arrest a murder suspect. The oppositions of the south-western desert landscape and the civilisation of New York retains the ideological structure of the classic Western: civilisation versus wilderness, masculinity versus femininity, religion versus pagan, etc., but reverses the meanings of the settings, with the progress of the original 'homesteader' having led to a corrupt, emasculated culture. The figure of Harry Callahan continues the theme of the outsider resisting the apparently illogical but inevitable culmination of civilisation such as civil rights, which are coded in the films as a form of restraining bureaucracy.

The libertarian ideology of the maverick cop films is evident in its reversion to the 'charismatic' legitimacy of the lawman, referring back to a time before the introduction of the rational legitimacy of the criminal justice system with its acknowledgement of the rights of the accused. This underpinning of the justice system was symbolised with the introduction of the 'Miranda' rights[1] in 1966, with the emphasis on the fair treatment of a suspect. The desire to return to an imagined time when issues of right and wrong had not been

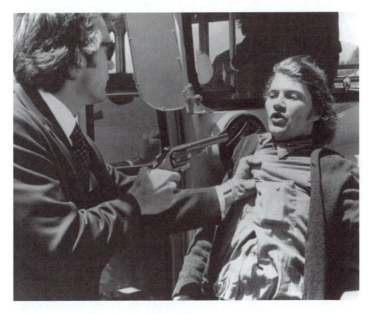

Figure 2.1 'I'm all beat up about that man's rights'. The maverick cop dispenses justice; Clint Eastwood as *Dirty Harry*

1 The warning read to suspects on arrest and includes the right to remain silent.

complicated by the law is represented in Harry's response to being told that he has violated a suspect's rights and that the case may not now be brought to trial – 'I'm all beat up about that man's rights' he replies sarcastically, summing up the film's viewpoint and audience position (a context which is used very differently in the film *Gone Baby Gone*, see Chapter 3)

Dirty Harry sets up the narrative conflict as not just between the policeman hero and the serial killer, Scorpio, but also between charismatic law and the criminal justice system, which is represented as absurd and an obstacle to justice. The representation of masculinity in these films is explicitly linked therefore to a specific ideal of the self-reliant outsider. This, in turn, effects a representation of women as either vulnerable victims who need to be protected in a paternalistic almost chivalric manner, or as dangerous and duplicitous. In *Dirty Harry*, Harry's actions, which go against the rules of the justice system, are always motivated by his desire to protect women and children ('a search warrant? There was a girl dying'). This characteristic is reinforced when Scorpio hijacks a bus full of school-children driven by a woman and Harry rescues them; his role as protector is symbolised by the repeated low-angle shots showing him looming above the action. The violence in the film is a precursor of the later 'cool violence' trend. It is accompanied by quips, performed without anxiety and without any of the later postmodern appeal to irony. Harry's gun, the iconic 44 Magnum, is brandished unselfconsciously as a phallic symbol, reiterating his powerful masculinity in opposition to the feminised, decadent serial killer he's hunting.

Kolker (1988: 50) argues that the violence in *Bonnie and Clyde* signalled a new development in the representation of violence in Hollywood. No longer would it have to be swift and quick, it could be drawn out – as with the 'do you feel lucky punk?' sequence in *Dirty Harry* – and anatomical. The relationship between audience and characters could be wrenched apart (a development begun with the death of Marion in *Psycho*) and it wasn't clear what the moral message of the film was any more. While Kolker characterises the violence in *Bonnie and Clyde* as representing the conflict between oppressive forces and those attempting liberation (the eponymous anti-heroes), he also identifies a paradox which, he argues, leads to a cynical glorification of violence. While the violence committed by Bonnie and Clyde has a liberating effect on the audience, the final violence done to them in a climactic, slow motion, cut-up sequence disrupts the viewer's pleasure by destroying the relationship constructed throughout the film. In this reading it isn't clear why Bonnie and Clyde's death is filmed in such a way. Is it a melodramatic 'compensating moral value' or the condemnation of everything the audience has been set up to admire in the rest of the film? Is it the triumph of form over content – the seduction of the image? For Kolker, the ultimate lack of meaning in the iconic scene of Bonnie and Clyde's death began the shift from violence as part of the narrative construction of the film to a function where form – the use of camera, the slow motion, use of jump

Figure 2.2   Liberating or cynical? A new tone in American cinema constructs screen violence as spectacle (*Bonnie and Clyde*)

cuts – took precedence over meaning, starting a trend for 'formal' violence most marked in the Westerns of Sam Peckinpah. This type of representation is controversial because it is cut off from a classical Hollywood narrative form of meaning and effect: 'violence is an easy way to command emotional response under the pretence of realism' (Kolker, 1988: 52).

The concerns about the effect of violent scenes on the audience, in Kolker's case the fear that it might have a brutalising effect, are similar to debates about the representation of sex on film. Like violence, it has been discussed in terms of moral instruction and as part of film form: the clichéd discussion about whether a sex scene is integral to the plot is delineating the same question about narrative imperative versus spectacle and titillation. Scenes of a sexual nature had been much more comprehensively cleaned from the screens than those of violence during the 1930s and 1950s, and for some theorists this was a form of sublimation: if there was no titillation then the audience could be brutalised through violence as a compensating sensation. This conception of sex and violence as performing a similar, physiological function for the audience laid the foundation for their similar depiction in the cinematic image – violence as pornography. The sensual pleasure of the violent image, which was foregrounded by the removal of the audience's alignment with character, was what made the new violence of the period so controversial. Violence was no longer a narrative part of moral conflict but was to be enjoyed and admired as spectacle, a sensuous, artistic pleasure. The changing function of violence from symbol of right and wrong – a punishment meted out to the deserving criminal – to the apparent glorification of criminality, achieved a new level of moral panic with the early films of Quentin Tarantino and the influence of his film style in the 1990s.

COOL VIOLENCE

The concerns about the representation of violence in American cinema in the 1960s, where the violent act seemed to be cut off from a wider contextual meaning, were revisited in the 1990s with a group of films variously named 'cool violence', 'new violence', 'the new brutalism' and 'neo violence'. As Gronstad (2008: 155) states, 'these nondescript labels are richly suggestive in that they underline both the extent in which the critics perceived the films in question to be genuinely innovative and the attendant lack of precision in signaling what the changes consisted in'.

The films which were seen to constitute this 'new violence' were a diverse range of mainstream and independent, genre and art house, auteur films and franchises which actually treated violence in very different ways but were linked by the fact of including explicit violence. They included: *Reservoir Dogs* (1992), *Pulp Fiction* (1994) (both Quentin Tarantino), *Natural Born Killers* (Oliver Stone, 1994), *Leon* (Luc Besson, 1994), *Fargo* (Joel Coen, 1996), *Grosse Point Blank* (George Armitage, 1997), *Romeo is Bleeding* (Peter Medak, 1993), and *2 Days in the Valley* (John Herzfield, 1996). There are some characteristic features which can be detected: the films are self-referential, commenting directly on the genre of which the film is part and parodying scenes from other famous films; they are hybrid genres and often experiment with classical Hollywood narrative structure; the soundtracks are often fashionably 'retro'. These distancing effects, which are characteristic of postmodern film production, contributed to accusations of a lack of feeling and character motivation, that the films were more concerned with style than substance.

The critical response was mixed in identifying whether these films were either a direct descendent of the new American cinema of the 1960s and 1970s (e.g. films by Scorsese, Peckinpah and Altman), continuing the tradition of reworking genres and film language to explore the lives of alienated characters, or a new type of film style characterised by a postmodern lack of meaning and emotion. The cynicism which Kolker identified in the representation of violence in the films of Penn and Peckinpah was now contrasted with the 'new brutalism' and found to embody positive values of humanity, loyalty and friendship rather than a celebration of violence for its own sake:

'One great difference between Peckinpah and his imitators lies in how deeply and passionately felt his violence is, and how securely it is tied to character, to milieu, to story – in a word to meaning' (Seydor, 1995). This re-evaluation of Peckinpah's work implies that the films of the 'new brutalists' have severed the link between cinematic violence and real-world meaning – and that this is inherently problematic.

This was also an accusation repeatedly aimed at the films of the Coen brothers. For some critics their oeuvre can be read as a long road towards showing that they feel emotion and have a moral sense (as seen in the near universal praise for *True Grit*, 2010), this perceived lack of feeling preventing their earlier films achieving greatness. While receiving a very positive critical reception, reviews for *Fargo* (1996) often referred to unease about the representation of violence which was usually based on a sense that it didn't 'mean' anything:

> *Fargo* contains some scenes of horrific violence, which feel all the more sickening against the mundane hyper-realism of the film's setting. This, clearly is evil, but what, exactly, is its source? . . . The first killing happens as a result of a dumb mistake, and the rest follow it in a chain of queasy inevitability, each crime making the next one inevitable.
>
> (Laura Miller, 2009)

In his *New Biographical Dictionary of Film*, Thomson (2002) evaluates the Coen's work in relation to how much genuine emotion and feeling they demonstrate. He sees *Miller's Crossing* as their most successful film to date (2002: 169):

> it had an emotional core which seemed to burn through the serpentine plot: here was a film about the difficulty and nearly the shame, in admitting feeling . . . had [the Coen's] at last found people to believe in and be moved by. Was that an aberration?

In mainstream film criticism the manner of the representation of violence is used as a value judgement, there is something lacking, immoral or at least distasteful about a film which does not use violence to make a moral point. This is clearly a subjective and culturally influenced interpretation, one which also changes over time as can be seen in the response to the violence in Peckinpah's films.

QUENTIN TARANTINO AND THE NEW VIOLENCE

The negative response to the directors associated with the 'new violence' of the 1990s reveals much about the understanding of film as a form and its expected function in society. The view of film as a form of mimesis is ingrained and one of the first signs of unease about the style of new film-making was its seeming distance from the 'real world', that these were films about other films rather than about life. With each level of removal from its referent in reality, the more disquiet the films caused. The cutting off from the real world meant, in this argument, the shutting off of alignment and empathy with characters, creating a desensitised response. In his review of *Pulp Fiction*, Lane (1994) argues that the director 'functions in a moral vacuum' and that he 'is an artist mad for affect, terrified that his audience may be bored or moved (the same thing as far as he's concerned)', comparing the use of violence in *Pulp Fiction* to that of *The Big Heat*, which, in contrast, is 'a moral furnace, stoked with such heat and vengefulness', in other words deeply felt emotion, which becomes a criteria of value in much of the response to the work of these directors. This approach accepts that films have a direct relationship to reality and the audience, downplaying cinema's role as an art form with its own constructed language. It also takes the opposing view to a dominant theoretical perspective of the 1960s and 1970s, namely that film must foreground its status as a construction in order to distance the spectator. In this analysis, distance from characters and plot was the only way to provoke an analytical response from viewers, not a brutalising experience.

A related way of interpreting this style has been to read the violence as a joke or to aestheticise it as stylish or 'cool', and it was this interpretation which provoked the most reaction from the regulators. James Ferman, in his final report (1999) as director of the British Board of Film Classification, commented on the 'drip, drip, drip effect' of 'designer violence':

> Too often in my view it functions like a drug, like a pounding beat of rock music which keeps the serotonin levels up. I worry that violence has so little meaning that younger cinema goers take the view that violence is cool, a view which seems to me to be simply an excuse for not empathizing with the victims.

His analysis once again views popular culture (music as well as film) like a drug, rendering the audience helpless to its built-in response. Both Reservoir Dogs and Pulp Fiction were passed without cuts and received an 18 certificate, although 3 seconds of film were 'reframed' for the video release to obscure the needle injecting heroin into skin. (Interestingly Ferman takes seriously the idea that film can have a powerful visceral response – something explored late in the chapter when considering the concept of affect and the cinematic image.)

These arguments are clearly played out in the controversy around Pulp Fiction's representation of violence. In this case the reaction was further politicised by the link to issues of race and language. Much of the attack on the film – and the film-maker – was the product of an attack on postmodernism, which was popularly seen as a movement which valued style over substance and meaning. The characterisation of Tarantino as a postmodern film-maker is based on the way he creates the diegesis: this is a recognisable but parallel world constructed through a variety of references to forms of popular culture. This pop culture iconography is fetishised to force the audience to consider it in a new way.

Definitions of postmodernism are subject to debate and controversy, however there are characteristics which have become accepted as signifying a postmodern text – and which are particularly applicable to film. This categorisation relies on the interrelated concepts of simulation, bricolage and intertextuality. All these concepts emphasise the 'ready made' nature of postmodern culture – the assembly of new texts from existing ones. It is this stylistic tendency which has led to readings of postmodernism as ahistorical. This interpretation argues that the lack of any history or context beyond the reference to other texts in the postmodern aesthetic results in a loss of meaning and analytical possibilities.

Postmodern characteristics are apparent in *Pulp Fiction* in the acknowledgement of film history through the references to and recycling of genres, narratives and visual styles. Intertextuality is evident in the construction of the plot, where the narrative 'old chestnuts' (gang member takes out the bosses wife and must not fall for her; a boxer past his best is bribed to throw a fight; hit men are sent on a mission) of B-movie history are re-told. Genre iconography from the 1940s – guns, black suits, briefcases, cigarette smoke, crimson red lipstick and nail polish – appear throughout the film but don't signify that the film belongs to a specific genre.

Individual characters are also linked to a specific genre or film style – even though the rest of the cast may not co exist within it. Mia (the wife of the boss – Marsellus Wallace) is introduced as a femme fatale, her entrance imitating that of Barbara Stanwyck's in *Double Indemnity* (Billy Wilder, 1944). She is represented in black and white fragments – black hair, trouser legs, ankles, mouth – and we don't see her face until the car pulls up at Jack Rabbit Slim's. Her role as the untouchable but irresistible wife also echoes the triangular set up of 1940s film noir. Mia is a failed TV actress whose cancelled pilot, *Fox Force Five*, is an example of Tarantino's references to invented cultural signs (Jack Rabbit Slim's, The Big Kahuna Burger) which are intertwined with examples of 'real' popular culture and people (*Modesty Blaise*, Douglas Sirk). Mia's ability to affect the film stock itself – she draws a square on the screen to illustrate her dialogue 'Don't be a square' – points to the increasingly slippery distinctions between reality and representation highlighted by postmodernism. Mia is a character constructed from the fragments of other imaginary characters whose back story is an invented (but real in the film) TV pilot for a series which never existed – in any context. These levels of referencing and quotation within a single character are reminiscent of *Breathless (À bout de souffle)* (Godard, 1959) and the way in which Godard constructs the character of Michel Poiccard (Jean-Paul Belmondo) a would-be gangster who imitates Humphrey Bogart.

The difficulty of defining postmodern style is evident in the differing claims for it as either oppositional to or part of mainstream culture; whether it is parody or pastiche. The mainstream tendency is pastiche – a visually exciting imitation of existing styles which remains superficial because it is divorced from wider contexts. It is this reading which sees the representation of violence as problematic because it exists on the same superficial plane as references to burgers, toe sucking and TV shows. The oppositional mode – parody – is also imitative but aims to evaluate and subvert the original codes or meaning associated with the imitated form. The oppositional tendency questions and challenges, attempting to construct new meaning through placing existing cultural styles and movements in new contexts. In postmodern cinema this could refer to the way that the intertextual mixing of genres (e.g. blaxploitation, gangster, musical) changes the meaning of the original representations (e.g. race and gender). The mainstream mode is merely an imitation or copy with nothing new to say. Whether a text is parody or pastiche they will share characteristics of style, form and content which operate within either the oppositional or mainstream mode.

The sudden shifts and contrasts in tone from suspense and violence to comedy and the banal in *Pulp Fiction* (and much of Tarantino's work) is another important borrowing from Godard – and the French New Wave. In 'The Bonnie Situation' Vince (John Travolta) accidentally shoots Marvin, the student who he and Jules (Samuel Jackson) specifically did not kill when interrogating Brad and his partners. The impact of the violence is undercut by humour – the gun unexpectedly goes off – and irony, as at that moment Vince is asking Marvin whether he believes that God controls people's actions. After the death in the car, Jules is more upset about the mess Vince has made in Jimmie's (a character played by the director) bathroom, more fearful about his reaction than the death of a young man. The most sustained period of suspense is during 'The Gold Watch' section when Butch (Bruce Willis) and Marsellus (Ving Rhames) are tortured in a pawn-shop basement by the owner and a corrupt sheriff – both of whom are drawn as stereotypical hillbillies reminiscent of those in *Deliverance* (1972). Even when the two men are gagged, bound, covered in petrol and blood, and while the threat of rape is clear but unspoken, the use of film language provokes comedy. This is achieved through the long takes, so long that they have the effect of an uncomfortable silence that someone in the audience will have to break, quite likely through nervous laughter. As the sheriff plays a game of 'Eenie Meenie' between the two men to select his victim, the camera remains on their faces capturing their intense concentration on the game and the moment of hope in Marcellus' eyes when he thinks he isn't 'it'. The contrast between the children's game, the gravity given to it and the grown, sadistic men becomes absurd and is part of the way (sexual) violence is linked to representations of masculinity in the film: the men are often victims, childlike and bewildered. It is characteristic of Tarantino's style of this period that the actual violence takes place off screen, behind closed doors or just out of frame. This technique allows greater manipulation of the audience whether through the anticipation created in the period before the violence or through the unguarded reaction (often laughter) to the unpredictable.

A similar technique is evident in *Reservoir Dogs* in the 'ear-cuttting' scene, as it became known. It was this scene which caused the most outcry and repulsion on reception – apparently leading to walk outs during public screenings (Clarkson, 1995: 179). It has also been referred to in criminal trials as influencing the accused: 'A sadistic gang of killers copied a horrific scene from the crime movie *Reservoir Dogs* to

Figure 2.3   The appeal of cool violence? Mr Blonde will torture Marvin, but how should the spectator respond? *Reservoir Dogs*

torture and murder their victim' (*The Sun*, 28 June 2000); youths on murder charge 'copied Reservoir Dogs' (*The Guardian*, 5 July 2000). This film – and this scene in particular – has also been the focus for developments in the critical and theoretical analysis of violence and its relationship to the spectator. This approach places the focus on film as a medium which is particularly effective in creating affect in the spectator, a physical, bodily reaction which is a marked shift away from the dominance of textual analysis and theories such as structuralism.

FILM VIOLENCE AND AFFECT

The development of an approach which examined the affective dimension of film developed out of a need to discuss the sensuous and tactile responses to film in a serious way. As in the quote from James Ferman above, references to film provoking a physiological response were usually found in the context of popular culture being discussed like a drug, used pejoratively to provide evidence that film was a feeling rather than a thinking medium. The concept of affect recognises the powerful response elicited by film but doesn't consider it in moral terms: '[film] is a vivid medium, and it is important to talk about how it arouses corporeal reactions of desire and fear, pleasure and disgust, fascination and shame' (Shaviro, 1993: viii) Rutherford (2002) characterises the privileging of pseudo-scientific rationalism over the visceral in film theory as somatophobic and argues that to really understand affect a somatic theory needs to be developed. The theory of somatophobia, or fear of the body, was developed by feminist literary theorists to demonstrate the cause and practice of domination by one group over another (see Spelman, 1990). Most usually the dominant group was white and male while the 'other' was female and/or black. The otherness of this group was demonstrated through the hierarchy of mind and body, the dominant group being linked to intellect and scientific thought while the inferior groups association with the body linked them to emotions, sexuality, hunger and instinct. This binary opposition has meant that affect in film has really only been discussed in the context of mass culture theory and the notion of the built-in response.

A somatic theory is clearly relevant to an understanding of violence in cinema as it can refer to the spectator's physical response to the somatic events on screen (such as the image of Mr Orange's bleeding abdomen, which is on screen for most of the duration of *Reservoir Dogs*). Gormley (2005: 8) draws on somatic theory when he argues that the films of the new brutalism 'all contain images which cause a reaction based on immediacy and bodily affect which subordinates critical consciousness and awareness of the world or knowledge outside its initial impact', and that this is a defining characteristic of this period of film-making, an attempt to 'reanimate' Hollywood film-making through affect. While this style makes the films controversial, it is also the way in which the film-makers subvert traditional forms and representations in cinema – particularly the representations of masculinity and race.

In an approach termed 'criminological aesthetics', Young (2010) combines the theory of affect with an academic background in criminology to construct an analysis of the crime film, specifically to explore the relationship between image, spectator response and societal views about crime and violence. In this analysis crime films represent our understanding of society, apparent in the way we choose to tell stories about crime, and also provide strong sensations and pleasure from watching violent scenes. In considering the workings of a scene of violence, specifically the way in which the spectator identifies with the illicit and the illegitimate, Young argues that the onus is on the audience to acknowledge complex responses to the act of violence, and not to just look away or to simply enjoy it. For Young, the ear-cutting scene in *Reservoir Dogs* provides pleasure for the audience but she also argues that it doesn't allow the audience an 'alibi' (or justification) for their response (Young, 2010: 30). She compares this scene to torture scenes in the TV series 24, which does provide an alibi or 'screen' – torture is necessary to save the lives of millions – and which is more dishonest in its relationship to the spectator. *Reservoir Dogs* is therefore a more truthful and even moral approach to the representation of violence, an analysis which privileges interpretation over the construction of meaning. The sequence, in a deserted warehouse, takes place after the heist has gone wrong (a result, the gang assume, of betrayal from the inside, most likely by an undercover police officer) and features Mr Blonde (who the audience has seen to be violent and out of control) and the policeman he has kidnapped in the hope of forcing a confession from him. The controversy provoked by the sequence is due to the mixture of torture, humour and the construction of the torturer as 'cool' as he dances to pop music while preparing for the violence. This combination of tones around a sadistic killer is iconic of Tarantino's style of this period. In her analysis, Young identifies three strategies in the sequence which she uses to generate her interpretation: the withholding of the most violent image – the actual slicing off of the policeman's ear – the pause in the intensity of the scene (for audience and victim) when Mr Blonde leaves the warehouse and goes out into the sunny parking lot, and, third, the construction of Mr Blonde as 'cool' as he dances to the soundtrack 'Stuck in the Middle with You'. These three strategies manipulate the audience and place them in a compromising position, both taking pleasure in the torture but also being horrified by it.

In addition to the strategies outlined above, other techniques are also used by the film-maker in constructing spectator response. A combination of restricted and omniscient narration, the framing of the shots and the editing of the film all work to manipulate and shift spectator alignment in relation to the violence. Audience knowledge at this point in the film means that they expect Mr Blonde to behave in a violent and uncontrollable way. This effect is reinforced by the dialogue: when Marvin (the policeman who is bound to a chair and gagged) with some bravado says Mr Blonde can 'torture him all he likes' as he doesn't know anything, Mr Blonde calmly states that he will torture Marvin for his enjoyment as much as for information and that Marvin's only hope is to 'pray for a quick death, which you ain't going to get'. Therefore the spectator has no 'alibi'; it is clear that a sadistic killer is going to torture an innocent police officer for pleasure and we can either watch (with a range of responses), close our eyes, leave the cinema or stop the film. The use of camera to position the viewer within the sequence echoes these possible responses, representing the discomfort of watching a Tarantino film. In the build up to the violence suspense is created. Marvin is going to be tortured it's only a question of when and how badly. During this part of the scene the camera moves around Marvin, following Mr Blonde's circling of the victim. The sequence is marked by jittery movements in the use of camera and in the performance of the actor playing Marvin. His head continually nods up and down and his shoulders twitch, reinforcing the nervousness and anxiety of the scene for the spectator. At this point the audience is aligned with Mr Blonde, cautiously following behind him, but the next cut repositions the spectator: rather than being in the warehouse with the men, the shot is composed as if Marvin is sat in the cinema row ahead of the spectator, emphasising the spectator's position as cinema viewer, distanced from the actions on screen and able to reflect on his/her response to what is happening there.

The spectator is continually shifted in their relationship to the on-screen events, which has the effect of replicating the ambivalence felt towards the on-screen violence. The film language contrasts long takes, fast-paced editing, long shots and close-ups in a way designed to unsettle the viewer, who seems to be urging the violence on and withdrawing from it simultaneously.

The question of alignment – how film-makers create particular reactions to a character through a range of techniques – is relevant here. Alignment can be created through the role played, the character's function in the plot, the character's personality and traits, the actor playing the role, camera positioning and editing. At the beginning of the sequence and central to its set up, the spectator is aligned with Mr Blonde, one of the main characters in the film and a central part of the group carrying out the heist. 'Why the heist went wrong' is the central narrative thrust of the film and Mr Blonde is engaged in finding the answer to that question. His actions in killing innocent bystanders in the aftermath of the robbery are terrible but he is also calm and collected in defending himself, realistic about the crime they have committed. The actor playing Mr Blonde (Michael Madsen) although relatively unknown before this film brings connotations of cool in his personae through references to rock 'n' roll and Elvis Presley. In contrast, Marvin, although the 'good' character, has barely appeared in the film until now, giving very little opportunity for the audience to align with him. This pre-existing situation, so important in manipulating spectator response, is countered by the film-maker through the use of point of view and shot reverse shot. Though the sequence starts with the spectator following Mr Blonde, many of the following camera choices are about an alignment with Marvin and a distancing from Mr Blonde. The only point-of-view shots in the sequence are Marvin's and they are used at the riveting moment of Mr Blonde's dance. The use of shot reverse shot, emphasising Marvin's bloodied, anguished face, means that the audience watches Mr Blonde's dance through Marvin's eyes, challenging the dominant interpretation that the viewer is removed from the horror of the scene to enjoy the moment of 'cool'. However, the most frequent spectator position in this scene is hovering over the shoulder of either Marvin or Mr Blonde, ultimately remaining complicit by accepting that position. Thus the spectator is aligned with the victim and the torturer at different times but ultimately takes up the position of bystander – or voyeur.

The most marked contrast in the style of filming in the scene is the use of static camera when Mr Blonde cuts off Marvin's ear. At the beginning of this action the camera is positioned behind and to the left of Mr Blonde, composed so that he is out of frame, placing the viewer very close to the action, peering in to look. The action continues but the camera pans to the left, seeming to look away from the scene of violence. The shot which follows is notable due to its static nature in contrast to the continual movement and restlessness of the previous scenes. Due to the way the camera movement and shot itself is foregrounded, the audience is very aware of the cinema apparatus at this point. The emptiness of the mise en scène – it is one of very few shots without any human figures – and the empty doorway adds to the confusing set up of space in the warehouse; the viewer has no comprehension of where the doorway might lead to.

The viewer is given a long time to contemplate this setting while listening to Marvin's screams, time to respond to the scene and to think about that response. This deliberate pause in which the filmmaker's presence is apparent accuses the spectator of both cowardliness and hypocrisy: we knew there was going to be torture so what impulse made us stay and watch? (We're not tied down like poor Marvin.) Although we can't tear ourselves away, we also can't watch the worst happen and we avert our gaze. Or by forcibly averting our gaze is the film-maker teasing us – you know you want to look really?

In this analysis of the cool violence in Tarantino's style there is a clear link to the way in which the themes and style of Hitchcock's films have been discussed. These films have been defended from accusations of titillation and misogyny with the argument that his films examine the relationship between spectator and cinema – with particular emphasis on the concept of voyeurism – rather than wallow in it. In this reading the shower sequence in *Psycho* (1960) becomes a punishment for the viewer, an attack on their desire to watch horror on screen. The subsequent alignment with Norman Bates becomes an exaggerated illustration of the spectator's own impulses in watching horror films. This theme is made explicit in *Rear Window* (1954) where L.B. Jeffries (James Stewart) spies on his neighbours in the apartment building opposite his, their lighted windows very similar to a cinema screen, with Jeffries sat in place of the audience watching scenes of relationships and murder. (In the teen crime film *Disturbia*, a loose remake of *Rear Window*, the young male hero actually makes popcorn to eat while spying on his female neighbour.) In both *Psycho* and *Rear Window* the camera movement is foregrounded at various times, becoming a presence in the diegesis. This can be seen in the opening of *Psycho*, when the camera pauses before deciding to go through a specific window, and after the shower sequence when the spectator is shown around Marion's empty motel room. In *Rear Window* the camera pans round Jeffries' apartment before pausing to stare at his sleeping face, and then moves outside once again. This spectator awareness of the apparatus and the presence of the film-maker is used by Tarantino in this sequence to similar effect, to remind the viewer of their role as a spectator of a constructed work of art and to question the impulses which make us want to and not want to watch.

VIOLENCE AND VENGEANCE IN KOREAN CINEMA

Recent discussion of the films of Korean director Park Chan-wook by critics, academics and the popular press reflect the continuing currency of mass culture and audience effects approaches to film violence. *Oldboy*, one of a trilogy of films exploring the theme of vengeance, provoked extreme responses – winning the Grand Prix at the Cannes Film Festival but receiving many hostile reviews – and was implicated in a 'copycat' crime. The plot of *Oldboy* centres on Oh Dae-su, an 'everyman' who has been imprisoned for fifteen years without explanation – for him or the audience. On his release – the reason for which is also unexplained – he is given money and a cellphone and a helper in the guise of a wait-ress from a noodle bar. Oh Dae-su's quest is to solve a series of puzzles: who imprisoned him and why; to find out who murdered his wife and to clear his name; to be reunited with his daughter; and to take revenge. This narrative structure has clear affinities with classic detective fiction and with the 'wrong man', mistaken identity films associated with the thriller and particularly Hitchcock (*North by Northwest*, *The Wrong Man*). *Oldboy* extends the themes of that sub-genre, questioning the innocence assumed by the heroes of such films and who, as agents of revenge,

Figure 2.4 'The use of violence as the great leveler between classes'. Oh Dae-su in *Oldboy* is characteristic of the revenge hero in Korean cinema

are long-established and celebrated figures in Korean national cinema. Central to the relationship constructed by the film-maker between the central character and the audience is the use of restricted narration: the audience is firmly aligned with Oh Dae-su, only discovering information about the past as he does.

Park Chan-wook's films foreground the implicit melodrama of the crime film in the use of coincidence and unexplained events, extreme emotion and anti-realism. The style of Park's films is based on hybridization, the visual style mixing references from film noir, graphic novels (*Oldboy* is an adaptation of a manga comic), surrealism and fairy tales. The structure and themes draw on Greek tragedy, parable and fairy tale, mixing comic book, black humour with extreme violence and other scenes designed to revolt the audience (most notably the eating of a live octopus in *Oldboy*). The combination of the tone and subject matter with the use of a rich colour palette and carefully framed compositions has been described as 'visual pyrotechnics' and led to familiar accusations of 'style over substance' and 'the stylisation of violence'. Manhola Dargis (2005) in a review of *Oldboy* places her analysis in the context of mass culture theory and postmodernism: 'The fact that *Oldboy* is embraced by some cinephiles is symptomatic of a bankrupt, reductive postmodernism: one that promotes a spurious aesthetic relativism (it's all good) and finds its crudest expression in the hermetically sealed world of fan boys.' She sees the film as symptomatic of an emerging theme in contemporary cinema, that of violence for its own sake and for pure pleasure, which is indicative of a morally bankrupt culture:

> In this world, aesthetic and moral judgments – much less philosophical and political inquiries – are rejected in favor of a vague taxonomy of cool that principally involves ever more florid spectacles of violence. As in, 'Wow, he's hammering those dudes with a knife stuck in his back – cool!' Or, 'He's about to drop that guy and his dog from the roof – way cool!' Kiss-kiss, bang-bang, yawn-yawn. We are a long way from Pasolini and Peckinpah.

Hendrix (2006) rejects this view of Park's work – and the work of other Korean directors – arguing that it is based on a misunderstanding of Korean cinema and that it must be analysed in the context of a specific cinema in a particular time. The vengeance trilogy is an example of national cinema exploring a 'distrust of authority [and] the use of violence as the great leveller between classes ', which combined with the melodramatic instinct 'makes for cinema that assaults sensibilities'.

This argument over the implications of violence in Korean films provides a concise summary of the opposing views of the meaning and function of violence in crime films. These are characterised by the argument that a popular audience can never be trusted to deconstruct violent scenes and will be affected negatively by viewing them; that film-makers have a duty to use violence responsibly to illustrate character and themes as an integrated part of the film rather than as spectacle. These differing concerns about the effects of violence are evident in the attempts to censor and regulate film as well as in the media assumption that violent films can lead to violent actions. The analysis of violence in crime films also refers to recent developments in film theory which emphasise the visceral rather than analytical responses to film as a neglected area of study.

3

NARRATIVE STRUCTURE AND NARRATION IN THE CRIME FILM

The function of the investigation

The nature of the stories told by crime films foreground a range of narrative elements in their focus on: the quest for knowledge, the gradual uncovering of information, and the primary importance of the analysis of events by the spectators. Theories of narration are particularly useful in anlaysing the crime film, in identifying characteristic structures and understanding how these structures construct a particular representation of society. The preoccupations of formalism and structural theory are also well suited to the study of the crime film, which often takes the most horrific and inexplicable of crimes and attempts to render them explicable through the use of repeated patterns and forms. In this chapter contemporary crime films including *Gone Baby Gone* (Affleck, 2007), *Zodiac* (Fincher, 2007), Hidden (Caché) (Haneke, 2005) and *The Secret in their Eyes* (El Secreto de sus Ojos) (Campanella, 2009) are discussed in the context of narrative theory. This approach illuminates how the crime film explores the human attempt to impose order on a world (the function of the investigation) which is beyond control. In the gap between this dream of control and the reality, the crime narrative works as metaphor for a range of moral, political and historical concerns. Dyer (1997) illustrates this approach in his analysis of serial-killer films. These include *Seven* (1995), a crime film which focuses on the extreme violence and cruelty that human beings are apparently capable of and pits that against moral, but ultimately powerless policemen (Morgan Freeman and Brad Pitt). Dyer argues that the pessimism and hopelessness of the story and its representation in a mise en scène of decay is countered for the audience by the structural form which actually provides reassurance in its use of convention and narrative predictability. These include the use of genre conventions in the hybrid form of police procedural and serial-killer film, the clichéd character of the detective counting down the days to retirement and taking one last case, and the pairing of an odd couple familiar from the buddy movie. The high-concept aspect of the film, the serial killer who kills to illustrate the seven deadly sins, is another example of repetition and predictability, each murder following a particular pattern. In this way *Seven* can be compared to the functioning of fairy tales, which often take the most gruesome events but package them into a manageable structure.

This brief summary of Dyer's essay illustrates some of the concerns of the dominant approach to narrative and narration in film studies. This approach conceptualises narrative as dealing with repetition and constraint: it performs a function for the audience of making difficult ideas and concepts manageable. In doing so, narrative cinema provides a reassurance that 'everything will be okay' but, it is argued, is unable to deal with contradictions encountered in social and political life. This type of structural analysis has focused on the function of mainstream cinema as a conservative force (see also the discussion of mass culture theory in Chapter 2) in comparison with avant garde cinema which was able to deal with complex and contradictory content. This analysis, framed in the opposition of realist and anti-realist cinema, sees narration and structure as part of the range of a film's formal elements which are key in positioning the spectator to accept a particular message. All of these elements of form in mainstream cinema work together to create a harmonious and concordant experience, a defining characteristic of the 'classic realist text' (MacCabe, 1981 [1974]). This style was seen – particularly in the politically conscious film theory of the 1970s – as inherently ideological and conservative.

NARRATIVE AND NARRATION

The terms narrative and narration are often used interchangeably but have specific meanings. Narrative in film refers to the elements which constitute the story, plot and characters; narration is the way in which those elements are communicated to the spectator. This includes the organisation or structure of the story, whether it is organised sequentially or in flashback, etc., as well as the formal and aesthetic elements of mise en scène, editing, framing and sound. The function of narration is not the objective recounting of a story but a way of constructing a viewpoint through which the film is received, to create engagement with the audience and, in classic realist texts, to convince the audience of the truthfulness of what they see. In mainstream cinema the construction of this viewpoint is often through the alignment with characters that reinforces the viewpoint of the film. The term narrative structure is used to refer to the way film narrative is organised into a specific form such as a beginning, middle and end, and is relevant to the work of structural theorists who have studied the ways in which different types of narratives conform to repeated patterns.

CONTEXT: MAINSTREAM NARRATIVE CINEMA AND IDEOLOGY

The history of the development of film form has tended to be seen as a series of inevitable technological advancements in the service of the drive to greater realism and immersive storytelling, the two being understood as inextricably linked. This includes: the development of continuity editing with its emphasis on cause and effect and temporal and spatial fluidity; the close-up, which provided the opportunity to study faces, character and emotions, in order to provoke empathy in the audience; the introduction of sound recording, meaning that complex plots and relationships could now be transmitted quickly and more literally than through inter-titles and symbolism; the development of colour, which meant that the world on screen was more recognisably like the real world than when it was represented in black and white (the recent development of new 3D technology could also be added to the list). In this account the technological and formal history of cinema is explained by the desire for a – debatably – more complex storytelling mode and verisimilitude. In this style, narrative is dominant over spectacle and is ultimately a form of constraint. There are, though, counter-voices to this argument, notably Gunning (1990), whose history of early cinema describes it as a 'cinema of attractions' where audience pleasure did not rely on the identification with character or the following of a plot. This concept of the disruption to narrative progression is also relevant to some of the approaches to writing about violence in the crime film (see Kinder 2001). The dominance of narrative cinema globally, backed up by the institutional dominance of Hollywood, has now left little room for non-narrative cinema, but in the 1920s experiments in film form – for example in surrealist films – were evident.

The importance of form and structure for theorists such as Wollen (1972) and MacCabe (1981 [1974]) was based on the understanding that form was ideological: there was a direct link between the way in which a story was told and its ideological position. In this context, structure and form is dominant over the content: there is no possibility of a narrative film containing a radical ideology, it will always reinforce the status quo. This analysis of Hollywood cinema in particular, and mainstream film-making in general, was defined as the 'classic realist text' and has the specific meaning of an ideologically conservative cinema which positions the audience to accept a single message. In the crime film the foregrounding of the way the story is told due to the emphasis on an investigation, can create a shift in the relationship between form and content which in turn comments on the classical Hollywood form. MacCabe defined the classic realist text in film as presenting the world in an unproblematic way to the viewer as truth through the narration. The classic realist text employs a hierarchy in which the spectator is given the privileged position and point of view: the camera reveals the world as it is, the classic narrative structure resolves all the problems, and therefore the passive spectator accepts this as truthful. Kolker (1983) identifies a similar style and function in his analysis of the form of Hollywood cinema – or degree-zero-style film-making – which was

> dedicated to a comfortable situating of the spectator's gaze in a cinematic world where space was whole and enveloping (even though it was made up, particularly in American film, of short, fragmentary shots), time complete and completed in an easily apprehensible order. Within this small but complete world the passions of both character and spectator would be large but manageable, directed in assimilable curves and, above all, predictable and resolved.
>
> (1983: 28)

Another way of analysing this type of film-making was through poetics as developed in *The Classical Hollywood Cinema* (1985/2005) by Bordwell, Staiger, and Thompson. Rather than an ideological account of mainstream film-making, the authors set out to identify the formal norms of film production from a particular institution at a particular time. These included the use of cause and effect as an overarching form of narration as well as a specific way of linking scenes and shots (continuity editing), a narrative structure which ended in closure and resolution and audience alignment with a goal-orientated protagonist.

NARRATION IN *GONE BABY GONE*

Gone Baby Gone is an adaptation of a crime novel by Dennis Lehane (whose books also provided the basis for *Mystic River* (Eastwood, 2003) and *Shutter Island* (Scorsese, 2010)). The story centres on the kidnap of a young girl, Amanda, and the investigation by private detectives, Patrick and his partner Angie, into her disappearance. It is firmly situated in a time and place: a working-class, post-industrial, suburb of South Boston in the early twenty-first century. The film conforms to the conventions of detective fiction with a restricted narration, an investigative structure which is propelled by the gradual revelation of information to the detectives and audience, including narrative twists and reversals. In addition to providing the pleasures of the detective form for the audience, *Gone Baby Gone* explicitly addresses one of the central concerns of the crime film: the moral choices involved in defining the difference between right and wrong, in this case placing the choice explicitly in the realm of moral philosophy. The film can also be read in a social and political context, telling

Figure 3.1   Shot composition demonstrates the growing estrangement between the detective (Casey Affleck) and his partner (Michelle Monaghan); the destruction of personal and professional partnerships is a recurrent theme of *Gone Baby Gone*

a story about the lives of a working-class community that is often marginalised or fetishised by popular cinema. The film's position on these issues can be analysed through the use of narration and the relationship constructed between film and spectator.

Formalist approaches to film narrative have been greatly influenced by the work of Tzvetan Todorov and Vladimir Propp. The structural analyses produced by these theorists were developed in literature rather than film, their subsequent application to film texts revealing both similarities and differences across the forms. In both cases the findings that popular forms were structured around repetitions was interpreted by those applying the model to film as ideological. These models were reassuring and hierarchical, emphasising, particularly in the work of Propp, the norms of hierarchical societal relationships and the drive towards marriage and family as resolution. The criticisms of these approaches have focused on the lack of textual specificity in the analysis which emphasises the similarity rather than differences between films and ignores the changing cultural context.

In *The Poetics of Narrative* (2006 [1977]), Todorov develops a theory of narrative typology drawing on the work of the Russian formalist Viktor Shklovsky and applies it to the novella form, specifically *The Decameron* by Boccaccio. The analysis is specific to literature, with the grammar of storytelling defined in relation to the differences between adjectives and verbs. Todorov provides a summary of the 'minimal complete plot':

> an 'ideal' narrative begins with a stable situation, which is disturbed by some power or force. There results a state of disequilibrium; by the action of a force directed in the opposite direction, the equilibrium is re-established; the second equilibrium is similar to the first, but the two are never identical.
>
> (2006 [1977]: 213)

This 'ideal' narrative is not the only possibility: a narrative may consist of only a portion of this ideal such as the passage from equilibrium to disequilibrium or its opposite. In a further categorisation

Todorov describes the stages of narrative in terms of two types of episodes which are either static or dynamic. The states of equilibrium and disequilibrium are static episodes which can be repeated indefinitely; the passage from one state to another is dynamic and occurs only once. In literary terms the first is the adjective, the second the verb. The application of this narrative analysis to *Gone Baby Gone* begins to indicate the view point of the film and film-makers.

Gone Baby Gone has an 'ideal' narrative. The equilibrium consists of a series of paired relationships: the child Amanda and her mother Helene, Patrick and Angie (professional and personal partners), Bea and Lionel (Helene's brother and sister-in-law, a married couple), and Remy Besant and Nick Poole (the police detectives who are investigating the case). The disruption to this equilibrium is the kidnapping of Amanda: this is a transgression against criminal law as well as against the understanding of the natural order of things, the primacy of the relationship between a mother and child. The state of disequilibrium therefore is Helene without her daughter. The transgression has other effects as well: conflict between Patrick and Angie, and Bea and Lionel, so that these couples are also in the state of disequilibrium. The film ends with a new equilibrium when the detective narrative is resolved as Amanda is found and the couples are all now separated.

The initial state of equilibrium is emphasised by the composition and framing of the different pairs during the first part of the film. The first meeting between Bea and Lionel and Patrick and Angie takes place when the former go to Patrick's apartment to hire them to look for Amanda. The discussion over whether they will take the case is framed in mid-shot and close-up with the two couples standing, facing each other. The shots cut from framing the individual characters to cutting between couples; each is given equal prominence in the discussion. This is particularly noticeable between Patrick and Angie, even as the conflict between them over their response to the case grows, as the formal grammar of the film gives their arguments equal weight in a series of level, shot reverse shot sequences. When Patrick and Angie, having agreed, reluctantly on Angie's part, to investigate the case, go to Helene's for the first time, the theme of pairs is continued: Patrick and Angie, standing, are placed in front of Helene and her friend Dottie who are sat on the sofa. The arrangement is deliberately unbalanced in the difference in height of the two pairs, but does not have the usual connotations that those sitting are inferior or disadvantaged. The emphasis instead is that both sides have strength in their partnership. This composition is repeated to a greater degree in the following scene. After a row with Helene, the original four talk in the hallway, repeating the earlier composition of the two couples facing each other. This is a pivotal moment in the narrative as Angie commits to the investigation, but does so due to her connection to Bea's loss (rather than Helene's) and this is reinforced by a change in the shot composition, as the sequence now cuts – without the characters moving – to position the two women on one side and the men on the other, emphasising the solidarity and sensitivity between the women rather than the heterosexual couplings. This shift in the previous harmony of the couple is a foreshadowing of the events to come and Angie's view on the preferred outcome of the case. The use of pairs to create meaning is continued in the first part of the film, such as in the scene when the private detectives meet the police detectives in a diner, but becomes disrupted thereafter, particularly as Angie begins to move away from the investigation and Patrick becomes a more conventional lone hero.

The setting of South Boston can also be seen as part of the equilibrium, the background of economic and social deprivation introduced as context and perhaps part explanation of the events of the narrative. The transgression of the kidnapping is presented as an attack on the community, where people take pride in their town as 'if it was something they had accomplished', as Patrick observes in his introductory voiceover. The gap in the community represented by the taking of Amanda has to be restored for the town to recover. This narrative of the damaged community pulling together is foregrounded in the mediation of the story by the local news media that repackage Helene, her friends and the people of the town into a recognisable and clichéd narrative.

In Todorov's analysis, a narrative has only two choices: to remain static or to progress. The logic of narrative with the disruption of an opposing force is that it must change and move forward to reach a new equilibrium. Therefore, in *Gone Baby Gone* the end cannot be the same as the beginning with its emphasis on the harmony of pairs against the backdrop of a struggling, close-knit city. As a viewer this creates certain responses. Knowing that the ending will not be a replica of the beginning provides a range of options for the narrative, such as that Amanda will never be recovered or that she is dead. Experience of watching popular cinema means that the latter option would be unlikely, as the death of a child is rarely used as a plot point due to audience sensitivities. The alternative, that Amanda may be alive but is never found, is also unlikely due to the lack of resolution it would provide to the main plot line. It would also represent the hero as a failure. The other options available to the spectator at this stage would be that the found child goes to live with her aunt Bea who loves her and misses her while her real mother neglects her – she was in a bar when Amanda was taken. For Bea to take the place of the mother, Helene would have to be removed from the narrative in some way or come to the realisation that her daughter is better off with Bea and Lionel, who can give her a more stable home. This would make Helene a tragic but noble figure in the narrative. A related but alternative new equilibrium would be that Helene realises that her behaviour has been selfish and that she must sacrifice her own needs for that of her daughter's. This resolution would conform to Todorov's alternative model of narrative structure where the equilibrium is brought about by adjective – changed character – rather than a verb, action. The actual new equilibrium of the film rejects all of these possible outcomes, thus producing pleasure for the audience in providing a narrative twist but also emphasising the specific viewpoint constructed by the rejection of other narrative alternatives.

As expected, the new equilibrium of the film is changed in many respects from that of the beginning. Patrick and Angie have split up, Lionel has gone to jail leaving Bea alone, and the two police detectives are dead. The static episodes, those that are the same at the end as at the beginning, are that Amanda has been returned to Helene, and the city continues on its way. The resolution of the plot provides a series of moral and legal choices for the characters and the audience. Their adherence to one or other of the choices renders them on the moral and criminal dividing line between right and wrong. Patrick finds Amanda after uncovering a complicated series of events characterised by accidents, good intentions gone wrong, as well as corruption and criminality. Amanda is safe and happy, living with Captain Jones (a respected police chief whose own child died) and his wife, who can give her love and provide the advantages of a middle-class life. Patrick insists that she must be returned to her mother and calls the police, acting against Angie's wishes. The debate between Patrick and Captain Jones draws on the didactic method – each character arguing their case for the audience. Jones is played by Morgan Freeman and his star persona of dignity, integrity and sympathy are deliberately chosen to make the decision all the more difficult for the audience. In addition, Angie's viewpoint – that Amanda should stay where she is – is given equal weight in framing and editing.

The narrative of the film has made it inevitable that Patrick will make this decision: whenever he is faced with difficult choices he always chooses the rigorous, moral option rather than the pragmatic one. For example, Bresant tells him how he planted evidence so that a father who he knew, but couldn't prove, was a drug dealer and guilty of abuse could be sent to prison and his son 'rescued', but he can't persuade Patrick that this was the right thing to do. For Patrick, the committing of a crime cannot be justified by the ultimate prevention of a greater one. (In this the hero of *Gone Baby Gone* makes an interesting contrast to the maverick cops of the 1970s, such as 'Dirty Harry'.) The film's viewpoint at this stage is that Patrick is right, taking the side of the marginalised and damaged characters, the new equilibrium emphasising their right to be treated equally. However, the meaning of the film is not only created at the level of narrative organisation but also through the micro-elements, which suggest a contradictory interpretation: that the hero's decision is the wrong one.

The opening sequence of the film functions conventionally, introducing the time and place, the central characters and the enigma. Like many other classic narrative films the opening is both part of the overall narrative and a micro-narrative of its own. The understanding of the beginning of a narrative changes throughout the course of a film as it is later understood in the context of the ending, which becomes inevitable in retrospect. The beginning of *Gone Baby Gone* lasts until the arrival of Bea and Lionel at Patrick and Angie's apartment to ask them to take up the case. During this time it introduces the audience to the different styles of film-making used in the film, the main characters and the plot. It also sets up the spectator alignment with Patrick and places the audience in a position of mastery over the material, in the way in which MacCabe (1981 [1974]) indicated is conventional of the classic realist text.

The film opens unconventionally in silence, a fade in on a low-angle, long shot of a row of typical Boston triple decker houses which fill the frame. This is followed by an urban landscape of factory buildings with the stars and stripes painted on one wall and then with a close-up of a man sitting on some steps, smoking, his face cut in half by the diagonal of the wooden banister. For the first time the camera moves, panning up the body of a young woman, showing her low-slung jeans, flat, tattooed stomach, floaty, flowery shirt, gold earrings and necklace. The woman suddenly turns, apparently in response to someone's call, and looks behind her before turning back to gaze out of the frame. The upwards pan of the camera is accompanied by the first sounds of any kind, non-diegetic, mournful piano music, its plaintive tone reinforced by Patrick's voiceover which is introduced shortly afterwards. The opening continues with a series of shots of the inhabitants of this place, again staring out of the frame – a father and daughter, an old lady and a dog – all placed on their front porches.

This sequence of shots follows a narrative logic, starting with shots of the city infrastructure, introducing the people who live there as a community or group, silent and part of the backdrop, then giving a voice – through the use of voiceover – to the central character Patrick, and therefore aligning the spectator with him from the start. The sequence continues in this way, accumulating detail and movement as it shows people playing baseball, having their hair done, laughing and joking. The film form of the opening uses documentary-style realism, an observation of the people of the town in their everyday, authentic lives (standing, staring, smoking, chatting, working and playing) and this style is used throughout the film – observational sequences which punctuate the detective investigation pausing the plot development.

The realist aesthetic of the credit sequence is reminiscent of the title sequence of the gangster film *Mean Streets* (1973) where the home-movie projections of city life make a direct connection between the city milieu and the behaviour of the characters. In *Gone Baby Gone* the form has a similar effect and it also acts as a guarantee for the audience of the verisimilitude of the narration. The voiceover introduces the themes of the film: the situation of the marginalised in society, 'the people who started in the cracks and then fell through'; the difficulty of surviving physically and spiritually in such a place where you have to be as 'wise as serpents' and 'innocent as doves'. The religious reference is reinforced in the shots of the church and in the characters' crucifixes, part of the context of the city. As Patrick speaks, the images of the inhabitants seem to illustrate his words – 'I always believed it's the things you don't choose which make you who you are; your city, your neighbourhood, your family' – creating a literal relationship between voiceover and image, reinforcing the truthfulness of the character's point of view. The audience seems to share Patrick's viewpoint, making links between the images, looking around 'our' city, the editing reinforcing these links through movement of the characters which smoothes the transition between shots.

Patrick's voiceover, 'I've lived on this block my whole life', places him as part of the city, but he is also clearly separate from it through his narrative position as hero, his superior economic and cultural position, and through his access to the spectator in the voiceover. Alignment with Patrick is not the same therefore as alignment with the people of South Boston. The documentary-style filming also adds to the distancing of the spectator from the people and the place: the emphasis on observation, with people unaware that they are being watched, places the spectator as voyeur. The audience also knows more even than Patrick: from an omniscient position the audience has knowledge of the town before Patrick arrives.

The simultaneous alignment and distancing of the spectator with the hero culminates in the positioning of the spectator in the new equilibrium and the understanding of the film's ideological message. The stasis of the new equilibrium is represented in the final scenes of the film. Patrick, alone now that Angie has left him over his decision to return Amanda to her mother, visits Helene. Helene is about to go on a blind date with someone who saw her on a TV show, *American Victim*, suggesting that her culpability in the initial loss of her child has not had any lasting effect on her behaviour. The final shot of the film is charged with meaning and undercuts the pure moral basis of Patrick's choice. Patrick, babysitting for Amanda so that she won't be left alone, is sat on one end of the sofa; Amanda, in a pose that has connotations of adult body language, is at the other end. The gap between them in the composition both recalls and denies the harmony of pairs at the beginning of the film. The mise en scène is cluttered, messy but not grimy, suggesting a chaotic not abusive household. The camera pans around the room, stopping to create a long, almost still, take of the characters on the sofa. The spectator is positioned behind the TV, which dominates the frame and the light from the screen is visible on Patrick's face. In this resolution two meanings are competing: Amanda should be with her mother; Amanda should be with the people who kidnapped her. The viewpoint of the film which is conveyed to the spectator in their omniscient position is that Patrick's choice is the wrong one, sending Amanda to a neglectful, limiting existence, represented by the desolate, uncertain image in which the main form of communication is with the TV screen.

The image crystalises other aspects of narration in the film. TV has been used throughout for different purposes, to impart information about the case to the spectator and characters but also as part of the representation of the culture of the community. In addition to the news reports and televised press conferences, *The Jerry Springer Show*, a gambling game and cartoons (the TV as babysitter) are selected to represent the cultural life of the characters. The way in which the media packages the story of Amanda's kidnap through the use of cliché and easy emotion reinforces TV as a medium of lies and malign influence.[1] The uncertainty of Patrick in this final shot recasts his earlier decisions. The number of times he has misunderstood a situation or been tricked by people cleverer or more manipulative than him – a tendency foregrounded by the 'false climax' two-thirds of the way into the film when the case appears to be solved – now seem to be indicative of a man who is out of his depth. The ending retrospectively shapes the beginning. Patrick's poetic voiceover now seems to be naïve and misplaced, the images contradicting not reinforcing his viewpoint, suggesting a more traditional filmic representation of the working-class community as corrupt, responsible for their own state of marginalisation. The new equilibrium of the film suggests that Patrick is as 'innocent as doves' but certainly not wise as a serpent, which leads to him repeatedly failing to do what he sets out to do and destroy the life of a girl.

The ultimate desolation of *Gone Baby Gone* is engendered through the techniques of narration conventional to the classic realist text: the audience as omniscient is positioned to accept the symbolism of

1   The condemnation of the medium of television in film is a familiar theme in cinema (see *Network* (Lumet, 1976), *Broadcast News* (Brooks, 1987) *The Truman Show* (Weir, 1997), etc.) and has much in common with the mass culture theorists. In this resolution it works to illustrate the film's message – that Patrick has made the wrong decision.

the image as dominant in film (see MacCabe's analysis of the final sequence of *Klute* (1981 [1974]: 56)). As a detective, Patrick has succeeded in solving the puzzle and restoring the loss of the girl, none of the elements of the investigation are in doubt. Instead, the anxiety felt at the end of the film is provoked by the responsibility of acting on the facts as they exist: how can Patrick ever know what the right thing is to do? In *Zodiac* the focus is on the impossibility of ever having certainty about events, actions and motivation. Here, instead of the characters and spectator making choices with god-like omnipotence, they are both left doubtful and anxious. In doing this, *Zodiac* is a deconstruction of the detective and police procedural film, challenging the reassurance and satisfaction which is more commonly associated with the genre.

FAILING TO SOLVE THE CRIME: *ZODIAC*

Zodiac is 'based on actual case files'. It follows the investigation into a series of killings which took place over two decades (the first was in 1969) in California. The case became infamous due to the nature of the killings themselves but also because the killer had constructed a persona, the 'Zodiac', and was taunting the media, specifically the *San Francisco Chronicle* newspaper, with a series of letters containing clues to his identity, often in the form of a cipher, and threats relating to his next acts. The film is based on the book by Robert Graysmith (1996), one of the 'amateur' detectives involved in the case (he was actually a cartoonist on the *Chronicle*), and details his quest to reveal the identity of the killer. While Graysmith is ultimately the dominant character in the film, there are three other detectives, an investigative journalist, Paul Avery, a police inspector, Dave Toschi, and his partner, Bill Armstrong.

Zodiac can also be situated as a 'David Fincher film', where the auteur structure intersects with genre themes and conventions. In this context, *Zodiac* can be compared most explicitly to *Seven*, with the shared subject matter of the investigation into a serial killer, an interest in subverting narrative expectations (in *Seven*, the serial killer gives himself up, denying the audience the pleasure of the detectives' triumph), and the exploration of male friendships and partnerships. Fincher's world view as an auteur accepts the uncertainty, often terror, of existence. This can be seen in *The Game* (1997) where Nicholas van Orton (Michael Douglas) is thrown into a terrifying and seemingly inexplicable sequence of criminal events which threaten his life. This experience turns out to have been an elaborately constructed game bought for him by his brother. On discovering that his experiences had not been real, Nicholas is devastated, not because of what he has been through but because the solution to the enigma has been denied: there never can be a satisfactory answer to the question. It is this concept which is the unsettling theme of *Zodiac*. The identity of the Zodiac killer has never been confirmed in the criminal justice system – the prime suspect died before he could be charged

Figure 3.2 Not solving the case: the professional (Mark Ruffalo) and amateur (Jake Gyllenhaal) detectives in *Zodiac*

– which means that there can never be a definitive end to the film. Like Nicholas in *The Game*, Graysmith is pursuing an ultimately hopeless quest for the truth. The lack of a satisfying resolution to the enigma may be one of the reasons that *Zodiac* did relatively poorly at the box office: in the US it took only half of its $65m budget at the box office (although based on a true story it is debatable how many of the target audience would know the outcome of even a famous case from twenty years ago).

The representation of obsession, time and transformation which characterises the chronological narration of the Zodiac case is also a theme of Fincher's films. The nature of the experience of time, how to represent something abstract as visual, is apparent in *Seven*. Here the emphasis is on time compressed: the countdown to a detective's retirement is symbolised by the ticking metronome in Somerset's apartment. This focus on time is characteristic of the crime genre, which features deadlines, the race against time, attempting to 'beat the clock', etc. In *Zodiac*, Fincher uses the representation of time passing to signify the helplessness of the characters in their attempt to solve the case, as well as demonstrating their insignificance within the context of the passing decades. For Wagner (2010), Fincher is 'exploring ways to represent time and timelessness in a senseless world'.

The sense of urgency and the anxiety of time passing are evident from the start of the film in the use of two subtitles, the first of many in the film. Recognisable features of the true crime genre in film and TV, subtitles are often used as a form of reportage, giving a guarantee of authenticity to the story. In *Zodiac* the sheer number of titles used throughout becomes almost meaningless to the audience as it is difficult to keep track of dates, times and places. In this way even the subtitles reflect the experience of the detectives who are overwhelmed by the amount of information they have to deal with. The increased appearance of the titles as the film progresses is also important in recreating the experience of time passing, suggesting it is a headlong rush rather than an ordered progression of manageable experiences.

Subverting the genre

As a crime film, Zodiac contains many typical features of the genre. These features are then subverted to construct the themes of the film. The film opens with a conventional pre-credit sequence which features predictable subject matter for the crime film, the murder of a young woman and the shooting of her lover, who is left for dead. Therefore the film sets up the required enigma, in this case, who is the killer? It also suggests the possibility that it might be the woman's jealous husband. The enigma of identity is reinforced by the first shot of the film, a point-of-view tracking shot from the driver's seat, as the car cruises along a typical suburban street lit up by fireworks for the 4th July celebrations. Withholding the identity of the driver creates the false assumption that it is the killer on the lookout for a victim, when it is actually the victim herself. This misdirection is both typical of the genre, the false plateau of suspense, but also provides the first suggestion that the attempt to identify the killer is futile. In this shot, the themes of the film, the need to know the face of the killer and the ultimate denial of that quest, are evident.

Two decisions about casting and narration in Zodiac are important in the development of the themes and audience response. The only crimes represented in the film are those which had eyewitness accounts, usually from a surviving victim, and the role of the Zodiac at these crime scenes is played by a different actor. The first decision has the effect of reinforcing the restricted narration: the film-maker cannot provide an omniscient position for the viewer which would give them a privileged position over the detectives. The second emphasises the uncertainty in the hunt for the killer's identity and the fallibility of memory – the eye-witness accounts give different descriptions. The effect of these film-making decisions are apparent in the first montage sequence which leads up to the third murder scene: the shooting of the taxi driver. The montage opens with the use of a title (a feature used repeatedly in the film) '2 weeks later – San Francisco, California, Oct 11, 1969' superimposed over what appears to be a helicopter shot of the city, giving the spectator a bird's-eye view of the city blocks and grid system, an omniscient view which is rarely used in the film. Immediately preceding this shot was the revelation of a clue, the reference to the film *The Game of Death*, which builds up the expectation that the investigators are in control of the case and provides a knowing context to the city montage. The montage soundtrack comes from a radio phone-in show with a variety of views expressed about the motivations of the killer and likely targets, while, simultaneously, the camera pans down the side of the buildings to pick up the man who is going to hail a taxi – the Zodiac. The taxi journey is filmed from above, tracking the car along deserted streets, the length of the sequence indicating its significance – the duration of the journey is hard to gauge due to the use of transition dissolves – and our privileged position in tracking it. That this is merely an illusion of omnipotence is revealed when the murder of the driver is from a witness's point of view, someone who heard but didn't see the murder. The montage sequence is a condensed narrative which distils the structure of the film, moving from an optimistic expectation of revelation to another dead end. The frustration is reinforced when it emerges that due to an error in the description of the suspect, two police officers let the Zodiac go.

The hero is introduced during the film's credit sequence which comes immediately after the scene of the crime and this is also conventional, making a connection between the crime and the hero who is going to solve it. Following the night-time scene of the killing, the hero appears in the morning, following his daily routine on the way to his job at the *Chronicle*. This organisation of events is again typical of classical narration, creating many expectations for the audience through the repeated patterns and forms used. Here the morning signifies the world as it is, a new day with the connotations of hope but also disruptions to come. By joining Graysmith on his way to work the audience is aligned with him from the start. As Graysmith is arriving at his desk so is the first letter from the Zodiac, the parallel editing charts the journey of the two and places the audience in an omniscient position. The explicit connection between the Zodiac and the hero is reinforced by the letter: as Graysmith is told to be 'in editorial in two', the audience is shown the hand-written instruction on the letter to 'Rush straight to the editor'. The two are being pulled together and this sets up the clear narrative expectation that Graysmith will solve the case. It also indicates that he will be the audience's main character alignment in the film.

Zodiac uses the genre convention of the 'buddy' film, a typical detective theme with the relationships of opposites shifting to mutual respect over the course of the narrative. There are two buddy relationship structures in the film, with Graysmith being the younger partner in both. The first is between Graysmith and Paul Avery, the investigative journalist who provides the world-weary, cynical contrast to Graysmith's more innocent and credulous worldview. In his partnership with the police detective, Dave Toschi, the contrast is also marked by the contrasting approaches of the amateur and professional detective: Graysmith's apparent solutions to the case are constantly overturned by the policeman's understanding and respect for the legal system. Graysmith and Toschi work together because they have both lost their previous partners due to the obsession with tracking down the Zodiac. (The characters that are discarded or destroyed by the quest for answers also include Graysmith's second wife and children; people disappear in the film but the need to solve the case remains.) In the final section of the film, Graysmith is working alone, with some encouragement from Toschi, who has been taken off the case.

This shift in the number and function of detectives in the film is part of a repeated formal structure which emphasises the narrowing of the focus of the investigation, from great to small, and in turn represents the effects of obsession over two decades. The film's narrative can be organised into three sections: the first is the relationship between the media and the Zodiac as he carries out his murders; the second shifts to the mechanics of the police investigation; while the third is Graysmith's lone pursuit, which is characterised by a series of breakthroughs and frustrations. The first and second sections detail the overwhelming amount of evidence the detectives have to examine, the number of people involved in the hunt for the serial killer and the failure of their efforts to produce a definitive result. The burden of evidence nearly destroys Graysmith: he is constantly seen rifling through papers, checking for references, scribbling notes, and at home the documents replace his family. The sacrifice of the family to the obsession of the investigation is both similar and different to the conventions of the form:

> Just as in the Western and gangster films of yore, home is the realm of normal reproductive sexuality at stake in the hero's engagement with the killer's abnormal, destructive world. He is protecting home from what the killer represents, doing his bit to make the world safe for women and children.
>
> (Dyer, 1997: 17)

Instead of the home being a sanctuary, Graysmith's apartment is represented as threatening and unsafe in the latter part of the film, when he repeatedly receives anonymous phone calls which he assumes are from the Zodiac. The theme of the contamination of the home is crystallised in a tense scene when Graysmith, hearing noises in the apartment, mistakes his wife for an intruder.

The obsessive hero vs. police procedure

Graysmith's final revelation, which convinces him of the identity of the killer, comes once he has to distil all the unwieldly evidence into a few lines. Given permission to go back and check some police files in Vallejo, Graysmith isn't allowed to make notes, instead he has to memorise anything important. When he has finished he rushes to a diner where he scribbles three points on a napkin – the narration of the investigation has moved from the universal to the specific, from an institutional procedure to subjective obsession.

The obsession that the detective in the crime film has to uncover the truth is a signifier of their morality: they are literally unable to do anything else because of their need to see justice done. It is also what makes them victorious. In Zodiac this idea is deconstructed. The film doesn't just suggest that the detectives may pay a price for their obsession but instead uses the investigative narrative to comment on the nature of existence, the futile attempt to control events and the ultimate impossibility of ever knowing the truth. This theme is developed in the way that the film subverts genre conventions. There is almost no interest in the victims in Zodiac, they perform in mini-plot sequences which take place away from the world of the detectives. The audience know nothing about them before they appear in their scenes as victims and hear almost nothing after their deaths (it is not even initially clear how many of the characters have survived the shootings) except as plot points in Graysmith's investigation. There is no recognition of the suffering endured by the victims, as in a film like Silence of the Lambs (1991) (which Zodiac does reference in a later scene in a suspect's basement), or evidence of the empathy of the detectives. This is not done to suggest uncaring or brutalised men but emphasises that the film is not ultimately about the search for a killer but about the nature of existence. In this context the victims are only important as structure and form, the conventions which can be employed for a wider purpose.

The representation of the victims also fits with the world view of the film, that the experience of life is random and chaotic, however much the hero tries to organise it into a manageable, predictable certainty. Dyer (1997) applies this to his analysis of the function of different types of serial-killer film. Seven and Copycat (Amiel, 1995) represent the 'longing for form and sense', providing it in a self-contained world which is governed by the form's demand for finish and completion. In contrast, a film such as Henry: Portrait of a Serial Killer (McNaughton, 1986) truly subverts this attempt to control and rationalise:

> It realises in macabre and terrible form, the quintessence of seriality, the soap opera, the story with no beginning and no end . . . it opens up the

spectre of endlessness, forever trapped by compulsions of serial watching, engulfed in repetition without end or point'.

This analysis of the link between form and ideology in the serial killer film applies equally to *Zodiac*. The increasing number of the Zodiac's victims over the two decades, which are hard for the viewer to keep track of, are part of the volume of clues and evidence which threaten to confound Graysmith and the other detectives. The size of the case as it develops is linked throughout with the passing of time, which is shown to be both quantifiable – the subtitles continue to keep track throughout of time passing – but out of control. The use of a montage technique is particularly effective in representing this. There are four montage sequences in the film, which start by representing the passing of hours, then months and finally a year. Two of the montages represent the detail of police work and the unfolding of an investigation. The first of these details the increased rapidity of the receipt of letters from the Zodiac – the writing and codes are superimposed over the detectives as they are continually hurrying through offices and labs, an image of the overwhelming nature of the case. Different voiceovers are used to speak the lines of the letters, reinforcing the mystery of the writer. Previously in the film, letters had arrived gradually and with filmic emphasis, but in this montage the reception of the sixth, seventh, eighth and ninth letters merge into a simultaneous representation of clues, evidence, investigation and confusion.

The more information is received, the more bewildering the case becomes. In the grammar of film the montage compresses time, it signifies time passing but also that nothing has happened (a sense reinforced by the decision not to visibly age the appearance of the main characters). The montage is an adjective rather than a verb, it pauses time while signifying years in minutes. It is therefore the perfect symbol for the experience of existence: everything and nothing is happening. The duration of the montage sequences decreases in inverse proportion to the amount of time represented. The final montage employs stop-motion photography to show the construction of the Transamerica Pyramid Building from foundation to completion in 1972. This visual representation of time rushing by is preceded by expert testimony that the new suspect 'is not the Zodiac' and followed by scenes of Lavery's decline through addiction and illness. The order of the events – another dead end, time passing, Lavery's increasing paranoia – illustrate the destructive effects of obsession.

The clues work to provoke audience response and this is central to the narration of the film. Repeatedly, a new piece of evidence will seem to predict the final breakthrough and triumph, only for the hope to be dashed again. The first cipher sent to the *Chronicle* is solved by a history teacher, then Graysmith researches codes in order to break the subsequent clues and each time it seems as if a another piece of the puzzle has been resolved, but there is no progression in the case. By the time Graysmith's children, who are also pressed into service as mini detectives, discover an overlooked code it has very little meaning. This structure of peaks and troughs is again conventional of the genre but part of the pleasure for the audience is the understanding that the enigma will ultimately be resolved. The narration relies on audience expectation formed through the familiarity with the crime genre to subvert the predictable resolution. Graysmith's ultimate belief that he knows who the killer is cannot be accepted easily by the audience; his arguments have been shown to be unreliable so many times before. In this way the audience is made to experience the same cycle of hope and despondency as the detectives, to wish for closure.

The representation of evidence as unreliable, even treacherous, is a symbol for the world view of the film, where the more the detectives cling to the rational, material evidence, the more ephemeral it seems. This is personified in the role of the expert witness, the handwriting expert from the Questioned Documents department, Sherwood Morrill. At the point that Detective Toschi and the audience are certain that he has identified the killer, the evidence from the handwriting expert contradicts this. This emphatic ruling is later questioned by another expert who disagrees with Morrill's analysis. Later on, Morrill's credibility is further undermined with the suggestion that he is an alcoholic and had been forced out of his job. Graysmith counters with the version of events provided by Morrill and the audience is once again left uncertain. Doubting the certainty of scientific proof is a condition of postmodernism which the crime film, with its emphasis on competing versions of truth, is able to encompass. The expert is initially set up as infallible: Toschi trusts him to confirm or deny that the killer of the taxi driver is the Zodiac and takes evidence to him to evaluate. A familiar, tense scene follows with the detectives waiting anxiously on the word of the expert. As the narrative progresses, this trust and faith is demonstrated to be misplaced. The narrative drive towards the discovery of elusive truth in Zodiac is an extreme version of retardation. Conventionally, retardation reaches a climax; here it remains out of reach.

Zodiac is a deconstruction of the idea that the investigation symbolises a mastery over chaotic events. This is reflected in the disclosure of the actual events of the police investigation which Graysmith has placed so much faith in. This revelation emphasises the random and accidental over the planned and strategic: the police have discounted 2,500 suspects because their fingerprints do not match one found at a crime scene, but there is little certainty about the validity of the print, follow-up calls weren't made, a suspect discounted by mistake. For Graysmith, one of the key pieces of the puzzle is provided during small talk he makes with the maid at a house where he is waiting to interview someone. Chance and luck govern the investigation as much as rational detective work.

The use of the familiar conventions of the genre – the investigative structure, the role of the detective, retardation – actually function to undermine the spectator and to create uncertainty and disquiet. Zodiac is not about the serial killer: there seems to be very little interest in his psychology and motivation, but rather the quest to solve a puzzle which will remain unsolvable. The Romanian film Police, Adjective (Corneliu Purumboiu, 2009) has a similar emphasis on the role of police procedure. Here, a very low-key investigative procedure is imbued with a similar function and meaning to the technologically sophisticated activities of the justice system in *Zodiac*. *Police, Adjective* can be defined as an example of the 'slow cinema movement' where the effect of boredom is deliberately used as a technique to engage the spectator by demanding a close analysis of the mise en scène to create meaning. *Police, Adjective* uses long takes, minimal action and, for much of the film, a compression between real time and screen time, to follow a young detective's investigation into low-level drug-dealing. The majority of the film focuses on the detective, Cristi, on his long periods of repetitive surveillance tailing his suspect around the streets of a small town. He is then shown hand-writing his reports, close-ups of his sentences are used to demonstrate their significance.

The use and meaning of words becomes central to the film and are a way of exploring themes which are similar to *Zodiac*: how can individuals make sense of the world and create order? More explicitly in *Police, Adjective* is the understanding that the police – as a symbol of the state – are a line between order and chaos. The legal system is an ethical framework which must be followed; it cannot, as Cristi would like, be moulded and interpreted based on personal morality. In the final section of the film, Cristi and his boss debate the merits of an undercover operation which might bring the results that Cristi's investigation has so far failed to deliver – the arrest of the dealer and user. Cristi's objections are due to the youth of the suspect and the minor offences he is involved in (smoking dope). In response, his boss argues, through analysis of the meaning of words which Cristi uses ('conscience', 'law', 'moral' and 'police'), to defend the position that any contravention of the law, no matter how well intentioned, is unjustified.

For Young (2010: 170), the effect of this focus on the functions of the legal system is to emphasise the importance of process and procedure in the face of violence. The painstaking efforts of Graysmith and Toschi, which do not culminate in resolution, are not pointless:

> Futility, then, is not necessarily about *failure*. . . . There may be no possibility of an end to violence, . . . but within the endlessness of the task of

the criminal justice there persists the process, and the way in which one is carried forward by the process, towards the impossible end.

The reliance on process as a defence against the dissolution of the border between the criminal and the law is central to *Police, Adjective*. The crux of the argument between Cristi and his boss is about the relative power of the law and the individual. The film comes down on the side of the law, despite the spectator's initial sympathy with Cristi and his world view. In *Zodiac*, Graysmith argues that 'just because I can't prove it doesn't mean it isn't true', to which Toschi replies 'Easy, Dirty Harry'. (During the Zodiac investigation the San Francisco police department has arranged a screening of *Dirty Harry* which Toschi leaves in disgust in reaction to the celebration of maverick techniques over procedural.) In *Zodiac* – and more equivocally in *Gone Baby Gone* – ethics trump the personal crusading zeal of the hero; the investigative structure is used to symbolise the desire for control and closure which is ultimately unobtainable by the individual.

The ideological function of the classic realist text is foregrounded and questioned in the crime film through the use of an investigative structure which no longer provides harmony and reassurance. The privileging of the visual, which reinforced the meaning of the realist text, is also in doubt, with the crime film questioning the reliability and authenticity of the visual evidence. In *Gone Baby Gone* the versions of the kidnap story provided by the media through images of the grieving and then joyful mother are repeatedly shown to be manipulations and partial representations. The idea that we 'cannot believe our eyes' is particularly resonant in a medium where, historically, the visual language of cinema has been central to the definition of film as an art form.

THE STORY OF THE CRIME AND HISTORICAL MEMORY

In this chapter the investigative narrative has been shown to perform a variety of functions. It offers intellectual pleasures for the audience, provides a framework to explore issues of morality and even represents aspects of human existence. Another role of the investigative crime structure is to symbolise memory, specifically historical memory, in films exploring post-dictatorship and post-colonial countries.[2] Hidden (Caché) and The Secret in Their Eyes (El Secreto de Sus Ojos) are two recent films which share a similar subject focus, the suppression of historical events during dictatorship, but represent it in very different ways. The critical reception of the films tended to value Hidden's open and ambiguous form over The Secret in Their Eyes' more conventional and closed structure. Both films use the generic conventions of the crime film to explore political and historical events but the balance of these elements is very different. Generic structures are central to the Argentinian film with its setting of a judge's office and investigators as the central characters; Hidden sets up an enigma and a mystery but adheres to very few of the expected conventions as the film progresses.

Hidden is a crime thriller which focuses on George, an arts journalist living in Paris with his wife and child, whose family comes under an unexplained threat with the arrival of several videotapes. These are anonymous surveillance tapes of the exterior of his apartment, an unfamiliar Paris street and the farmhouse where he grew up. The investigation of the enigma of the tapes leads to the remembering and recognition of an event from his childhood in 1961. George's family had provided refuge for a boy who had been orphaned by the massacre of Algerian pro-independence protesters by the French police. Jealous of his claim on the family's affections and, it is implied, disturbed by the otherness of the Algerian boy, George persuades his parents to send the boy away, betraying him and ruining his future. The anonymous tapes implicitly accuse George, forcing him to

2 The workings of memory and its use as a metaphor for historical events is a central concern of European avant garde film movements of the 1960s. For example, see Alain Resnais' Hiroshima Mon Amour (1959) Last Year at Marienbad (1961) and Chris Marker's La Jetée (1960).

acknowledge the repercussions of his actions. The visual style of the videos is similar to surveillance or cctv footage, fixed cameras, long takes, no editing. It has minimal intervention from a film-maker and seems to have no point of view, the power of the image is to say that George has been revealed, made visible. The lack of explicit resolution to the question of who is behind the camera, who is sending the videos also confounds the expectations of classic narrative and the crime genre, conforming instead to the conventions of art cinema.

In *Hidden* the enigma of the video tapes is structured to represent the colonial and post-colonial relationship between France and Algeria (and post-colonial relationships more generally). George's comfortable, liberal intellectual life masks the past of France as an oppressive regime which was guilty of torture and murder. The subject of *Hidden* is the refusal of colonial powers to recognise their past and the devastating effect that has on both the perpetrators and more importantly the victims. The mise en scène of George's flat and workplace represent his life as walled in, protected but also isolated by shelves of books and films, the very things which are supposed to provide enlightenment and understanding. George's attempt to remain 'hidden' is what

Figure 3.3   The mise en scène of the liberal intellectual is a mask for past crimes in *Hidden*

makes the surveillance videos so menacing as they show his life in plain view, the dominant figure of the Western male is now the focus of the investigation. The level, unwavering gaze of the camera is dominant, George reacts to it but there is no interaction. Part of the discomfort created is the way that the character who is usually the subject of the film, male, middle class and white has become the object.

The role of surveillance and technology in contemporary society is a repeated theme of Haneke's films (*Benny's Video*, 1992, *Funny Games*, 1997 and 2007). Osterwiel (2006) discusses how this theme is explored from the first image of the film, which is from the first surveillance tape (although the spectator is unaware of the status of what they are viewing) of George's home on the Rue des Iris: '"Rue des Iris" may indeed conjure up an image of a street filled with flowers ... but in Haneke's oeuvre, it may more obliquely signify a "sadness of eyes," or the pain associated with looking. Extended vision promises knowledge, but knowledge, as Haneke will soon demonstrate, may be inextricable from individual and collective culpability.' In *Hidden* the atmosphere of dread and anxiety for the characters comes from being forced to look and to acknowledge culpability. A similar feeling is constructed for the spectator by the refusal to solve the enigma of the crime drama which is set up at the beginning of the film. The central character is terrorised and guilty but there is no closure to the events of the past. In an allegorical reading of the film this would be impossible due to the continuing iniquitous relationship between the 'post-colonial' Western and Arab worlds. *The Secret in their Eyes* shares with *Hidden* the use of allegory to discuss historical events, but provides a very different, ultimately uplifting analysis. This is evident at the level of form and genre as well as in the characterisation; here the hero is morally good and imbued with the near magical qualities of intuition recognisable from traditional detectives.

The Secret in Their Eyes is set in two time periods, the 'present' of Argentina 1999 and the past of 1974, the beginning of Argentina's 'dirty war'. Dirty War was the term given to the decade of military dictatorship characterised by widespread corruption and repression, including the use of torture against opponents. This period of state-sponsored violence led to the 'disappearance' of thousands of Argentinians; the fate of many is still unknown. The question of how a nation should deal with the trauma of its past is again presented allegorically in the film. Here the focus is an investigation into a past miscarriage of justice caused by state corruption and the film argues that remembering the past is imperative to the forming of a just society. The pleasures of the film are much more conventional than those provided by Hidden as the film conforms to genre expectations and constructs an emotional response by aligning the spectator with an appealing hero.

The first images of the film set up the spectator's intense alignment with the hero, Benjamin Esposito, a retired investigator for the court in Buenos Aries. The opening is set at a train station and shows a farewell between a man and a woman. It is presented as fragments in close-up and often filmed in slow motion; the distortion of the film stock adds to the sense that this is a subjective recollection and presentation of events. The revelation that it is Esposito's memory (he is attempting to write a novel about his past) reinforces the subjectivity and sense of partial recollection. To an even greater degree than the narration in Gone Baby Gone, the spectator is restricted to Esposito's world view as shaped by his memories, which may or may not be reliable. This position of reliance on the hero's understanding of events is further complicated by the fact that he seems to have very little understanding of his own feelings and motivations. In this, of course, Esposito is a typical hero of popular cinema in general and the crime film in particular. Espositio is a familiar detective archetype: he is dogged, reticent, an outsider driven by the need to see justice done. He also has hidden depths, he is a sensitive, artistic man who listens to classical music and is writing a novel. He is also loyal to his alcoholic partner Pablo Sandaval, another typical character of the genre, a helper who isn't as clever or charismatic as his boss. As the opening continues the crime story is introduced. This time it's Esposito's imagining of another man's memory, that of

Ricardo Morales, whose fiancé's rape and murder is the case which obsesses Esposito for twenty-five years.

Flashback and historical memory

The story of The Secret in Their Eyes is organised in flashback and this has a narrative and symbolic function. The contemporary scenes are a series of conversations between Esposito and his ex boss, Irene Hastings, which take place at her office, in cafes and finally at Esposito's apartment. These meetings emphasise the development of the love story which runs parallel to the investigation of murder and corruption in the film. The structuring device of the pair's conversations also dramatises the two alternative futures for Argentina posed by the film. Espositio's need to excavate the past, to find answers and to see justice done is continually countered by Irene's need to repress historical memory. For Irene, returning to the past is impossible:

Figure 3.4   The good detective (Ricardo Darin) has to fight a corrupt system which continually threatens to overwhelm him in The Secret in their Eyes

'I can't look backwards', she tells Esposito, arguing that Morales did receive 'some justice' and that this should be accepted in order to move on in life. In contrast, Esposito is like Morales, they are 'stuck in time' unable to move on.

As a judge, the character of Irene is a symbol of the laws which were passed in response to the end of the 'Dirty War'. Her decision to close the Morales case, to sign and seal the files, is emblematic of the laws passed to prevent the prosecution of the junta for crimes against humanity in the mid-1980s. The 'Full Stop' Law (Ley Punto final) of 1986 was brought in after some of the military dictatorship had stood trial and been imprisoned, the 'some justice' urged on Esposito by Irene. A different approach, based on investigation and recognition of the suffering of people during this period, had initially been brought in by the Alfonsin government, elected in 1983. The 'Never Again' (Nunca Mas) Report, produced by the National Commission on the Disappearance of Persons, investigated the cases of thousands of unexplained disappearances and contained an individual report on each case. In *The Secret in Their Eyes*, Esposito is writing his own Nunca Mas, attempting to discover what happened in the past and also to honour the dead. Esposito represents the world view of the film that individuals and countries can only recover by examining the past, despite the traumas which it will inevitably provoke. This view is reinforced in the characterisation and narration of the film.

The movement from present to past ignores the twenty-five years which Esposito spent in Jujy, a provincial town he escaped to when his life was threatened. This period is presented as a kind of limbo; it's only the process of investigation and remembering which is active and meaningful. In this the film is reminiscent of the gangster film *Once Upon a Time in America* (Leone, 1984), which uses the same interweaving of past and present in telling the story of a man, Noodles (Robert de Niro), whose life appears to stop when he is betrayed by his friend. He also goes into a self-imposed exile (for 30 years), propelled back to New York by the need to remember and investigate the past, to find out what really happened.

The Secret in Their Eyes does accept that there are aspects of the past which will never be known, such as the fate of the disappeared, and that the guilt ordinary people feel about these crimes has to be annulled. The murder of Sandoval is pivotal in exploring this idea. Sandoval is murdered in Esposito's apartment and it is assumed to be a case of mistaken identity. Esposito is guilt-ridden by his partner's death and imagines his final moments, creating a heroic narrative for Sandoval in which he sacrifices himself to save Esposito. This guilt has prevented him from visiting Sandoval's grave or mourning his death. In the move to resolution in the final narrative stages, Esposito takes flowers to the mausoleum where Sandoval's ashes are, finally able to forgive himself and to acknowledge that he doesn't know what happened to his partner – and that he must live with that.

The detective's intuition and the reliability of evidence

The title of *The Secret in Their Eyes* , in a similar way to that of *Hidden*, suggests that the past can never be entirely repressed, but will continually return until it is addressed and resolved. Unlike *Hidden*, *The Secret in Their Eyes* is much more confident that such a process can take place, that there can be an agreement about what the past means and what it represents. The differing approach to the interpretation of photographic evidence in the two films is symptomatic of this. In *Hidden*, images are treacherous, a site of ambiguity and threat. Esposito, in contrast, finds the solution to the crime in a photograph and never doubts this interpretation. During the initial stages of the investigation, Morales makes Esposito look through his photo albums in an attempt to make his murdered fiancé, Liliana, more real to the investigator. The photos are a record of their relationship and have been categorised and indexed; a key pins down the identity of everyone in each shot, a precaution against forgetting. While looking through these images Esposito identifies the murderer, Gomez, through the look in his eyes as he stares at Liliana. Throughout the film Esposito reiterates his belief that guilt is never erased, it can always be seen in a person's eyes. As a process of investigation this is farfetched but functions as an allegorical device for discussing the concept of a nation's guilt. In response to this discovery, Irene, reading Esposito's novel, argues that sometimes it is better not to look, but the narration of the film makes it clear that this is wrong.

The film's contention that the past continually interweaves with and shapes the present illustrates Walter Benjamin's concept of the woof and warp of memory and forgetting:

> When we awake each morning, we hold in our hands, usually weakly and loosely, but a few fringes of the tapestry of a lived life, as loomed for us by forgetting. However, with our purposeful activity and, even more, our purposive remembering each day unravels the web and the ornaments of forgetting.

> (Benjamin, 1992 [1929]: 198)

This link between past and present is evident in the filmic techniques used to represent the shifts in time. The flashbacks are not signalled by the use of transition devices (fades, dissolves, etc.) or a subjective voiceover from the central character, all techniques which represent the past as separate to the present of the film. In *The Secret in Their Eyes* the past and present merge, and it is initially difficult to distinguish which period the film is in (the characters are aged slightly but remain very similar to their younger selves). The movement in time is done by linking objects in the mise en scène: the kettle which links the shift from Morale's kitchen in the past to Esposito's in the present; the faulty typewriter Esposito used as an investigator and is now typing his novel on.

The composition of shots and the use of mise en scène creates an atmosphere of claustrophobia which represents Esposito's struggle to find out the truth in opposition to the official version. He is repeatedly positioned in darkness and often becomes an insignificant figure that can only just be picked out in the frame. The use of perspective and foreshortening exaggerates this sense, making Esposito seem vulnerable and alone. Another pattern of the visual style is the way large parts of the screen are obscured. This is often achieved by filming from behind a character, placing the spectator at the scene but with a restricted view. Esposito is often positioned behind the towering piles of paper files on the desk in his office, a visual representation of a justice system which is out of control and liable to crush him. The consistent visual style of the film is reminiscent of Expressionism. This is apparent in the use of low, canted-angle shots, the emphasis on a highly controlled mise en scène which includes chiaroscuro lighting and the dominance of interior settings. The reference to Expressionism is relevant to the film's themes of discovering the truth beneath surface appearances. Expressionist style, which emerged in German silent cinema, attempted to represent the reality of experience, not through a superficial realism but by revealing the underlying experience of the world. The link between expressionist style and the representation of contemporary society as a form of insanity (see The Cabinet of Dr Caligari (Wiene, 1920), Metropolis (Lang, 1927)) further emphasises the film's analysis of Argentina during the 1970s.

THE DETECTIVE NARRATIVE: OBSESSION AND RETRIBUTION

The heroes of Gone Baby Gone, Zodiac and The Secret in Their Eyes all share an obsessive approach to the investigation which becomes all-consuming in their lives. The investigations are used to explore themes of morality and fairness, in The Secret in Their Eyes this is focused on the debates around retribution and justice. The concepts are given historical weight by being part of the debate about which method is most effective in addressing Argentina's past, another reference to the idea of the two alternative futures for Argentina. The investigative structure creates a parallel between Esposito and Morales: both act as detectives with Morales carrying out his own investigation into the rape and murder of Liliana. The two men discuss the nature of justice and while both reject the death penalty Esposito does so because he believes it to be morally wrong, while Morales is convinced that it is too swift and not equivalent to the suffering that the murderer has caused. The crime narrative provides a metaphor for the experience of the population during the Dirty War. This is evident in the horrific violence of the crime and the emphasis on the goodness, beauty and innocence of the victim (she is a young, in love, a school teacher), as well as the initial attempt by police to frame two foreign suspects by extracting false confessions. Esposito's triumph in identifying and bringing the killer, Gomez, to justice is short-lived. Gomez is released from jail partly because he is useful to the government but also in order to punish Esposito for accusing a senior policeman of corruption. The narrative functions as a reminder of the effects of a government which no longer adheres to laws and which is rife with personal vendettas and corruption, the terrorizing of its population.

In Esposito and Morales' debate on justice, the fear of what retribution can do to survivors is unspoken. Morales' increasingly frail and desperate appearance suggests that retribution is highly damaging. The comparison and contrast between Esposito and Morales reaches a climax with the final resolution of the enigma at the end of the detective narrative. Morales has carried out his wish to make Gomez suffer, keeping him imprisoned in a make-shift cell in the basement of his house for the last twenty years. The horror of this revelation is compounded by the way that Gomez and Morales are linked by framing and mise en scène. Both are framed behind bars, looking almost identical: balding, frail, old men. In contrast, Esposito has escaped and is free. The mutual destruction of Morales and Gomez is a warning against the desire for revenge and an argument for justice and resolution. In *The Secret in Their Eyes* Irene is persuaded to Esposito's view. 'It will be complicated', she tells him in the joyful resolution of the film when they agree to be together, reflecting an optimism about the future, despite the obstacles, which is in great contrast to *Hidden*.

In telling the story of the crime and the investigation, crime films create a structure which functions as a predictable narrative pattern for the spectator. This ingrained pattern then allows for the experimentation in form as well as the exploration of difficult and controversial themes. The figure of the investigator remains central to this structure, functioning as a moral guide with whom the spectator is closely aligned and understands the world through. The detective narrative itself is closely associated with the portrayal of memory and it is this which allows it to encompass the diverse representations of conflict between individual and state morality.

4

CRIME AND SOCIETY

Ideology and genre

Ideological readings of the crime film have focused particularly on the gangster film and film noir. As discussed in Chapter 1, the character of the gangster has been read as a validation of individualism and entrepreneurship; representing a specifically American, capitalist ideology. This chapter examines the ideological function of the crime film when it deals with crimes in the public and private sphere, within the institutions which represent these areas: the family and the government. These examples of crime films range from the overtly political subject matter of the Hollywood crime thrillers of the 1970s (often referred to as conspiracy thrillers) and the hybrid form of crime melodrama. Both these cycles have provoked opposing readings, as conservative and progressive in the context of ideology.

THE POLITICAL CRIME FILM: NEW AMERICAN CINEMA IN THE 1970S

The crime genre deals both explicitly and symbolically with the conflict between different societal groups. It is therefore logical that the crime film's relationship to the society which produces it has been debated in political and ideological terms. The terms of the debate can be found in the analysis of political crime thrillers of the 1970s. This group of films, referred to variously as 'conspiracy thrillers', 'neo noir' and 'political thrillers', seemed to mark a shift in tone, subject and form in Hollywood cinema which led to differing interpretations of the films as either reinforcing or disrupting dominant ideology. The films most commonly referred to as comprising this sub-genre are: *Klute* (1971), *The Parallax View* (1974), *The Conversation* (1974), *Chinatown* (1974) *Three Days of the Condor* (1975), *All the President's Men* (1976). This group of films also belong to a wider category of New American Cinema (sometimes referred to as the American Renaissance or New Hollywood). The institutional, social and cultural background to this period of more experimental film-making is useful in understanding the political crime thrillers of the time.

In the 1960s the Hollywood studio system, still dominated by the institutions of the 'golden age', was on the verge of financial collapse. Following the post-war boom the studios now faced a series of regulatory and competitive obstacles. These included the divorcement of the cinemas from studio ownership and the introduction of television. Hollywood's response was defensive, adhering to a high-risk blockbuster strategy which relied on high box-office returns from big-budget films (a tactic which is still dominant with the reliance on 'tent pole' film releases). The downside of this strategy was evident in the late 1960s when Fox studios was nearly bankrupted by a series of high-budget flops such as *Dr. Dolittle* (1967) and *Hello Dolly* (1969). The traditional form and content of these films also demonstrated how out of touch the studios were with the emerging youth market. This was a much more counter-cultural segment than the studios were used to catering for. The disastrous reliance on the block-buster trend was underlined by the success of two medium-budget films which were unexpected hits due to their appeal to the youth audience: *Butch Cassidy and the Sundance Kid* (1969) and *MASH* (1970) (For more detail on this period of Hollywood production, see Schatz (1993).)

The shift in audience tastes led to a series of temporary changes in the way Hollywood film was produced and distributed: the block-buster trend was halted, the importance of the youth, rather than an older or family, market was recognised and film production reflected a more experimental approach to form and content. Biskind's oral history of the period, *Easy Riders, Raging Bulls* (1998), interprets the period as a panicked reaction on the part of studio executives to financial disaster, rather than an ideological response to the dominance of conservative values in Hollywood cinema. The film-makers are seen as motivated and excited by the possibilities of experimenting with form and content but this does not exist in any coherent political context. Biskind (1998: 22) quotes film-makers from the period, such as Paul Schrader: 'Because of the catastrophic crisis of '69, '70 and '71, when the industry imploded, the door was wide open and you could just waltz in and have these meetings and propose whatever. There was nothing that was too outrageous.'

The film style of this period can be characterised as a meeting between European art cinema and genre film-making (films by Antonioni, Roeg, Fellini, Godard and Truffaut had received wider distribution in the US in this period than had previously been the case). Typical conventions included an experimentation with narration through the use of ellipsis, flashback and non-linear narrative, a more improvisational, immediate style through the use of hand-held camera and natural lighting, a focus on the marginalised and anti-heroes who couldn't conform to society's expectations (*Easy Rider*, 1969, *Point Blank*. 1967). This content was personified in the emergence of new stars such as Warren Beatty, Jack Nicholson, Donald Sutherland, Jane Fonda, Julie Christie, Jill Clayburgh and Karen Black who brought a range of political or alternative personae to their roles. These more alternative aspects of film form and style were countered by the use of genres such as the Western, road movie, detective thriller (e.g. *Butch Cassidy and the Sundance Kid*, 1969, *Badlands*, 1973, *Five Easy Pieces*, 1970), which provided a more familiar structure to counter the alternative world view. This hybrid form of experiment and convention illustrates one of the reasons that the films of this period have been read as both alternative and conventional.

WHAT IS A POLITICAL FILM IN HOLLYWOOD?

The attempt to read Hollywood cinema as a political cinema (or to attempt to make political films within the studio system) has been controversial, some would say impossible:

> Films with an overtly political theme have always been distrusted by the major studios for the understandable reason that most of them . . . are box office failures. But if the political pill is sugared – and the framework of the thriller can often provide an effective sweetener – directors can score their political points without alienating either the studios or the audience.
>
> (Davis, 1973: 55)

The nature of political film-making has been discussed at the level of institutional context, form and subject. Central to the Marxist-influenced film theory of the 1970s was the argument that only a radical production context form could represent a radical message. Therefore as a capitalist system it is impossible for Hollywood to produce a film which attacks its own system of production. At the level of content, the political crime films of this period were attacked for their lack of realism in promoting a hero who would provide a solution to a problem (corruption in the system) which was much greater than acknowledged – the 'few bad apples' explanation. In this argument Hollywood films were incapable of dealing with the underlying structures such as inequalities of class, gender and race, which reveal the workings of society.

For Kolker (1988: 240) the films of this period were part of the 'shudder that went through dominant ideology in the sixties and seventies, beginning with the assassination of Kennedy and ending with the liberation of Vietnam in the late seventies'. This 'shudder' is marked in cinema by 'images and narratives of despair and impotence . . . and powerlessness'. This message of helplessness is, he argues, one of the reasons for the failure of these thrillers as political films: they are unable to analyse or promote social action, the plots erupt in violence instead. Kolker's analysis argues that these films provide an ideological reflection of the confused political discourse of America during this period, but that they are not radical or subversive. He characterises them as either liberal (the political thrillers of New Hollywood) or conservative – *Dirty Harry* (1971), *Walking Tall* (1973) and *Death Wish* (1974). Due to the ideological hegemony of American politics the two categories of films share many ideals and can co-exist with very little conflict: 'Both ideologies are centred upon the image of the male individual and his unfettered advancement in a "free enterprise" economy. Both are anti collective, anti female, anti left, hierarchical, and aggressive' (Kolker, 1988: 240).

Maltby (2001: 362) analyses the relationship between Hollywood cinema and political content within the context of the conventions of Hollywood film style. In this analysis the ideological purpose of the political film is to bridge the gap between the 'utopian' lives of the characters on screen and the reality of the audience. This means that questions of realism are irrelevant in evaluating the political content in Hollywood:

> *My Man Godfrey* (1936) invited its middle class audiences to imagine what the Depression would be like if it took place on the studio back lot where events were played out according to the conventions of a screwball comedy . . . *Mississippi Burning* (1988) . . . invited its audience to imagine institutionalised racism as if it could be solved by the conventions of a detective story.

This is not to attack Hollywood production for how it addresses such issues but to recognise that this is the form it takes: any political subject will be 'mediated by systems of conventions'. In this argument Hollywood politics are not irrelevant or trivial but operate within a parallel universe which is still recognisably like the audience's. This world is not in any sense 'realistic' but still powerful. This power is found in the way that films

> affect the circulation of those preoccupations of ordinary life by providing us with structures of thought and feeling, "pictures of probability", and shapes that we can give to experiences outside the movie theatre . . . They are the most ingrained aspect of Hollywood's politics.
>
> (Maltby, 2001: 363)

The opposing views of the effect and significance of political films in Hollywood has been characterised as the 'Costa-Gavras debate'. Costa-Gavras is associated with mainstream films, often thrillers, which have an overt political subject matter such as Z (1969) and Missing (1982). His films have been used to illustrate one side of the debate, namely that political films need to be in a mainstream form which the audience can engage with. On the other side of the debate is counter-cinema, where film-makers such as Jean-Luc Godard argued that only a cinema which rejected conventional funding, distribution and form could be political, the alienation of the audience was part of that process. Hill (1998: 115) outlines the key arguments held by opposing positions:

> For supporters of political thrillers, their great strength was their ability to both reach and to maintain the interest of an audience who would normally be turned off by politics; for their detractors, the weakness of such films was that their use of popular forms inevitably diluted or compromised their capacity to be genuinely politically radical to stimulate active political thought.

Lev (2000: 49) also points to the conflict between political subject matter and generic conventions:

> These films use the detective or mystery genre to offer an investigation of what is wrong with contemporary America. The conspiracy film's social

critique is often muted by or in conflict with genre requirements, but the willingness to critique such institutions as capitalism and government gives these films a liberal or Leftist slant.

CONVENTIONS OF THE POLITICAL CRIME THRILLER

The conventions of the films associated with the New Hollywood are apparent in the political thrillers under discussion here. All use the classic narrative of the investigative structure but with an emphasis on pessimistic or open endings. While not as formally experimental as some of the films of this period they are characterised by the use of ellipsis and montage which disrupt the narrative flow. Derry (1988: 270) places the conspiracy thriller in the 'innocent on the run' category, privileging the narrative form over the content: '[it is] organised around an innocent victim's coincidental entry into the midst of global intrigue', where 'the victim often finds himself running from the villains and the police'.

The subject matter of the films includes the explicitly political, such as corruption at government level which leads to assassinations and cover-ups. Government agencies such as the FBI and the CIA are named as the location of this corruption in some of the films (*All the President's Men, Three Days of the Condor*), in others it is a shadowy and mysterious corporation (*The Parallax View*). *Klute* and *The Conversation* use the tropes of surveillance and spying to construct an atmosphere of paranoia and helplessness rather than a specific conspiracy plot line. The narrative of institutional corruption is fairly widespread during this period with films such as *Coma* (1978) exploring similar themes in the context of organ trafficking in a hospital and *The China Syndrome* (1979), which investigates safety in the nuclear power industry. In all the political crime films the hero is conventional: male, young, white, attractive, but often powerless and doomed to failure.

The lone hero

The investigators of the political crime film are print journalists (*All the Presidents Men, The Parallax View*), private detectives (*Chinatown*), a policeman who is 'freelancing' (*Klute*), a CIA operative (*Three Days of the Condor*) and a surveillance expert (*The Conversation*). The official detective is rare and the character of John Klute is associated with more conservative and traditional values than the heroes of the other films. The typical protagonists of the political thriller signify to a greater or lesser extent the counter-cultural tendencies of the new audience (even when the hero is a CIA employee). This is evident in their appearance, 'long' hair, jeans, etc., and a lifestyle which is often sexually promiscuous and always lived close to the edge of mainstream society. This aspect is emphasised when the hero is played by a star such as Warren Beatty (*The Parallax View*), whose persona informs the reading of the character. Joe Turner (Robert Redford) in *Three Days of the Condor* is represented as semi-detached from the CIA, the mise en scène of his life representing that of an academic as much as a government agent. The fact that his job entails discovering the hidden meanings in books and newspapers mirrors the concerns of a conspiracy theory and also signifies the character as an outsider. In *The Conversation* the alternative nature of the Harry Caul character (Gene Hackman) is represented through his love of jazz and isolation. All the central characters share the traditional characteristics of the crime film detective: they are motivated by moral imperative and cannot do anything but investigate the crime. Most of the protagonists are also failures in this attempt; they are duped by people smarter and more powerful than themselves, leading to the distinctive pessimistic endings of the films.

The protagonists of the political crime thrillers are male and the representation of women is indicative of the contemporary social and cultural standards. There are a few films of the New Hollywood which do feature central female investigators such as *The China Syndrome* (Jane Fonda) and *Coma* (Genèvieve Bujold) but in *Klute*, Bree

Figure 4.1 'A naive belief in the power of the hero', in *Three days of the Condor* the hero (Robert Redford) is furtive rather than triumphant.

Daniels (Jane Fonda) is the object of the investigation. The women in the political crime thrillers – when they feature at all – appear in the traditional roles of love interest, helper, wife and tragic victim. In *The Parallax View*, the character of Lee Carter fulfils all three character functions. Lee is a TV reporter, signifying the 1970s mainstream feminist image of an independent career woman, and is introduced in the film reporting on the soon-to-be-assassinated Senator's visit to Seattle. Her commentary on this event focuses on the appearance of the Senator's wife and her interview is flattering and non-inquisitive. Three years after the assassination Lee is convinced of a conspiracy and that she is next in line to be killed; she is now stressed and terrified. Her next appearance in the film is on a table at the morgue after being found dead from a drugs overdose. It is Lee's death and her suspicions about the assassination which finally provokes the hero, Joe Frady, into action; Lee has very little meaning to the narrative in her own right.

The crime: conspiracy

The criminal investigation in the political crime thrillers is usually set off by a murder or disappearance. The inquiry into the original crime leads to the uncovering of further crimes and ultimately a conspiracy. This conspiracy is in place to obscure a greater, often state-sponsored crime. The audience is positioned to accept the truth of the protagonist's fears through a combination of alignment with the hero and omniscient narration. The hero is never an extremist who could be accused of being deluded; instead they are often part of the establishment who have to be convinced that there is something to investigate. In *The Parallax View*, Frady is dismissive when Lee, a fellow journalist and ex lover, warns him that their lives are in danger; he argues that he believes the findings of the government report into the assassination, that there was no cover-up. In contrast, the audience is clear that there was a conspiracy because of the narration. The spectator is shown what Frady could not see, that the suspected assassin was innocent. This initial resistance on the part of the hero is part of

Figure 4.2 'The open spaces of the city are threatening . . . it is dangerous to be in plain sight'. Modern architecture dominates the characters in *The Parallax View*

the convention of the crime genre but also has the effect of reinforcing the probability of the events. The audience is urging the hero to believe in the conspiracy so that it no longer seems farfetched.

It is the framework of the crime which refers to contemporary political and sometimes social and cultural issues. All the films reference Watergate. This is done in various ways, from the overt dramatisation of the investigation into the Nixon administration in *All the President's Men* to the pervasive themes of distrust in government and institutions in the films generally. The revelation via Watergate, that the US administration was spying on its own citizens, is reflected in the atmosphere of paranoia in the thrillers. The magnitude of this betrayal and its effects is symbolised by intimations of insanity, that it will send people 'mad'. Watergate and its aftermath is also referenced in the repeated images of surveillance which are used in the films. In *The Conversation*, Harry Caul is a surveillance expert for hire, a man who spies on people for money rather than ideology; the opening of *Klute* plays out over the close-up of reel-to-reel tapes, used for the surveillance of phone calls. Throughout the films, characters fear that they are being watched and recorded, fears that are never clearly distinguished from imagination. At the end of *Three Days of the Condor*, Turner disappears in to the crowds in a doomed attempt to avoid surveillance by his enemies in the CIA. The apotheosis of this insidious effect of surveillance is in *The Conversation*, where the hero is driven insane by the thought that someone has bugged his apartment and is listening to him. At the end of the film Caul is warned by phone that 'they are listening'; in response he searches his apartment to find the bugging device. The search begins meticulously and rationally, treating the process as another job to be carried out. As the search continues (the sequence lasts about six minutes during which time there is no dialogue) Caul becomes increasingly desperate and irrational, tearing wallpaper and knocking through walls. Caul's inability to find the bug or to know for certain that it exists acts as a metaphor for the altered relationship between individual and government. Cover-up

Figure 4.3   The hero is defeated by paranoia and despair in the conspiracy crime film (Gene Hackman in *The Conversation*)

and conspiracy results in suspicion and mistrust which is ultimately a form of stasis and inaction.

Open endings

The political crime thrillers are unusual in the context of Hollywood film style due to their lack of certainty and resolution. In this they are a precursor to the similar tone of the contemporary crime films discussed in the previous chapter, but here it is used to make an explicitly political – rather than personal – point. This is particularly evident in the downbeat endings in which the hero often fails in his mission. It is this disruption to the expectations of classic narrative which was the basis for much of the interpretation of the political thrillers as serious, realistic films, providing the link to a political reality: 'Conspiracy films . . . are unusual in American cinema in their withholding of a happy ending. The explanation may be that the moment of the Watergate hearings was so grim that a few Hollywood films departed from the recuperative, happy ending tradition' (Lev 2000: 50). The endings range from the ambiguous to the clearly pessimistic. The latter is exemplified by The Parallax View and Chinatown.

In The Parallax View, Joe Frady (Warren Beatty) is investigating a political assassination which he believes to be part of a conspiracy orchestrated by the powerful Parallax Corporation. The events of the film clearly refer to the assassinations of JFK and Robert Kennedy. The killing itself takes place in the restaurant at the top of the Seattle Space Needle, a waiter is seen running from the scene while a girl in a polka-dot dress can be glimpsed, all explicitly referencing the footage of the Robert Kennedy assassination. The aftermath of the assassination, with the setting up of a Commission to investigate the murder, is a direct link to the Warren Commission and the accusations that it was part of a cover-up of the JFK assassination. It has been suggested that the character of Lee, Frady's ex lover and a TV journalist, is based on an actual reporter who investigated the assassination and died from a drug overdose. The repeated allusions to real events constructs a representation of the American state as inherently corrupt and even murderous; it is a state which cannot be altered by actions of an individual. At the end of the film, Frady is a victim of the Parallax Corporation, murdered and framed as an assassin, unable to act in the face of injustice.[1]

The impotence of the usually active hero is also evident in the celebrated ending of Chinatown. The disagreement between writer and director of the film over the choice of ending illustrates the wider debates about the aims of the conspiracy film. The 'original' version, by the scriptwriter Robert Towne, ended with the villain of the film, Noah Cross, a corrupt businessman guilty of incest, being killed by his daughter, Evelyn, the lover of the hero Jake Gittes (Jack Nicholson). The murder is motivated by revenge and the need to protect her child, born as the result of Cross's sexual abuse. This resolution, despite the elements of tragedy, did have a notion of restorative justice: Cross has

1 These themes are also the basis for Arlington Road (Pellington, 1997), an explicit updating of the political crime thriller in which Jeff Bridges suspects his neighbours of terrorist activities.

been punished and cannot continue to abuse those around him. In the final version, Noah Cross survives, Evelyn is killed and Cross is seen leading their daughter away, getting access to her for the first time. These events are watched helplessly by Jake, his powerlessness emphasised by the fact that he has been arrested and handcuffed. Lev (2000: 59) argues that it is the use of the second ending which gives *Chinatown* the power to transcend its genre framework:

> If Cross is killed and the threat is ended, then *Chinatown* becomes simply a genre piece where evil is overcome by good, as in the Western, the detective story, and other genres. But if Cross wins, then the conspiracy of the rich, the conspiracy which runs America, is presented as all-encompassing. This is a terrifying vision appropriate to the dark moment of Watergate.

However the political analysis attributed to these endings is still debatable.

The unconventional representation of the hero and the pessimistic tone of the films are, for Kolker, part of an avoidance of the real injustices in society and a symbol of defeat: 'in response to feelings of social impotence, the subject as effective agent in cinematic fiction was diminished physically, emotionally and politically' (1988: 242). In this view the political crime films only offer a counsel of despair which reinforces the prevalent view that there is no point trying to change the system. The final line of the film, 'Forget it Jake, it's Chinatown', is the dialogue equivalent of a shrug of the shoulders, suggesting that a corrupt society is a naturally occurring structure which can't be altered (in this example it also draws on racial and cultural stereotypes such as Orientalism) and lends a more conservative slant to the film than might first be apparent.

More examples of ambiguous endings are found in *Klute* and *Three Days of the Condor*, both of which use the gap between what is said and what is seen to create uncertainty for the audience. The ending of *Three Days of the Condor* can be seen as a bridge between the nihilism of *The Parallax View* and the greater optimism of *All the President's Men*. In *Three Days of the Condor* Turner is on the run after discovering conspiracy and murder which is being carried out on the orders of the CIA. In this case it is done to cover up the plan to invade the Middle East in preparation for the oil supply running out in America. The conspiracy is justified by the conspirators as an example of *realpolitik* in contrast with the idealistic notions of their left-wing opponents. The CIA chief, Higgins, represents the first position, Turner (reinforced by the star persona of Robert Redford), the latter. In the concluding scene, Turner has once again narrowly escaped a trap set by Higgins intended to kill him. Standing on a busy New York street they debate the rights and wrongs of the conspiracy with Turner repeatedly arguing the moral imperative while Higgins argues that it is a matter of pragmatism: Higgins' detachment in referring to the 'games' that the CIA play demonstrates the liberal world view of the film. Turner accuses Higgins of not understanding what truth is, but rather a concept he does not find relevant or useful. The establishment is represented as treating citizens like children: the important decisions have to be made for them. This opposition culminates in Turner's revelation that he has told his story to *The New York Times* (the scene takes place outside its offices). This recuperative moment, where the action of the hero is backed up by the integrity of the fourth estate, is disrupted when Higgins introduces a note of doubt into this ideal: 'How do you know they'll publish it?' he asks, making it impossible for the hero or the audience to believe in this outcome with certainty. The final shot of the film reinforces this with Turner disappearing into the city crowds, furtive rather than triumphant. The image freeze-frames abruptly, an ending of panic rather than reassurance. The resolution of the film is neither recuperative nor entirely hopeless, but does imply that the belief in the power of an individual hero is naive.

The final sequence of *Klute* has been the subject of much discussion in the context of the classic realist text (see MacCabe, 1981 [1974]) where it was used to illustrate how the visual aspect of film was dominant in creating meaning. In *Klute* the murder and conspiracy narrative has been resolved before the final scene. This is unusual in this cycle of films but is consistent with the dual narrative of *Klute*, which is as much about the developing romantic relationship between John Klute (Donald Sutherland) and Bree (Jane Fonda), a prostitute and sometime drug addict. Klute is instructed to investigate the disappearance of a friend, Tom Gruneman, by Gruneman's business associate, Peter Cable. The conspiracy in *Klute* is the cover-up of a series of murders committed by a member of the establishment by using an innocent man as the fall guy. The framework of the story is very similar to other more political conspiracy films – the use of wealth and power to commit crimes, the price paid by the innocent citizen – but here the crimes are individual rather than corporate or institutional. The enigma of the film is solved by Klute, who discovers the fate of his friend Tom and is able to catch and punish the guilty man. Although he was initially deceived by Cable, he triumphs in a way that Joe Frady and Jake Gittes do not. The unsettling atmosphere of the film, which allows it to be grouped with the more overt conspiracy thrillers, comes through the spectator's uncertainty about character identity and motivation. Even Klute, the reticent, conservative and moral hero, is undermined by the perspective of the film. The title suggests the story is from his point of view but it is Bree whose interior world the audience has access to. This undermines the otherwise substantial, patriarchal representation of the policeman. The elusiveness of meaning culminates in the ending in which Klute and Bree are shown packing up the latter's flat in order to leave New York together. On the soundtrack, Bree is in conversation with her therapist (the film is punctuated by these sessions in which Bree discusses her conflicting emotions); the voiceover is uncertain as Bree states that she is leaving with Klute but also that she'll probably be back 'next week'. This disjunction between sound and image has led to the film being interpreted in conflicting ways. It can be read as either a conservative reinforcement of patriarchal values where Klute has rescued the damsel in distress, or an acknowledgement of the impossibility of Bree, an independent, city living, working woman conforming to the demands of the happy ending.

Lev (2000) also points to the brevity of this period of pessimistic endings in the cycle with political thrillers becoming more hopeful in films such as *All the President's Men*. Here the film does provide a recuperative ending as the journalist heroes do solve the problem and the guilty are punished.

The city

The city setting of the political crime thriller is one of the most recognisable conventions of the genre. As discussed in reference to the crime films of the 1930s, the city is not an innocent setting but reinforces the anxieties of the contemporary political situation. Cities in these cinematic representations are glamorous but dangerous; they provide a sense of anonymity for those being pursued but are also a site of alienation. In some of the films they signify disease and corruption. New York (the setting for several of the films) with its then reputation for economic crisis, civil unrest and high crime and addiction levels, along with its futuristic architecture (the World Trade Centre opened in 1972), embodies the representation of the city at this period. In the right-wing vigilante films of the time, identified by Kolker (1988), the city is frequently referred to as a cesspit or 'diseased', the view in the conspiracy thrillers is more ambiguous.

The mise en scène of *The Parallax View* is striking in its conception of the experience of the city, represented through iconic buildings (the Seattle Space Needle provides a Hitchcockian setting for the first assassination), glass and steel office blocks, hotel lobbies and convention centres. The glimpses of open spaces such as the park and the tourist train where Frady meets informants are subtly coded for the spectator as unsafe. When Frady first has suspicions about the conspiracy behind the Senator's murder he meets with an ex-FBI agent friend and takes a ride on a tourist train, a precaution against being watched. As the journey continues, the camera tracks back from a medium close-up of the men talking to a long shot, as if the men are being watched from behind a tree in the park. Despite the distance from the subject, the sound remains at the same level, creating the impression that the men's conversation is being recorded. The meaning of this shot remains ambiguous: is the spectator taking on the point of view of the conspirator? The uncertainty reinforces the sense that the open spaces of the city are threatening, that it is dangerous to be in plain sight.

The schema of lighting and setting in *The Parallax View* often reverses conventions: the bright, open spaces, whether natural or manmade, are the source of threat and deception; the dark and gloomy, small spaces are places of comfort and authenticity. This is set up in the opening, pre-credit sequence set at the Space Needle. The building is an iconic, futuristic design; its clean white lines are sharply composed against a striking blue sky and the sweep of the city skyline beyond. It is a modern setting, connoting progress, new technology and the optimism of the period in which it was built. In placing the assassination and conspiracy here the film shifts the city from a symbol of optimism to having connotations of paranoia. The mise en scène provides an ongoing reference to the contradiction between what is visible and the reality of what is happening: the cover-up. This is apparent in the setting of the assassination and the death of the supposed assassin. As it happens in the open there seems nothing to hide, making the accusations of a cover up seem more extreme.[2] The use of brightness to signify danger culminates in Frady's murder, which takes place against a sudden blinding light.

The use of setting to indicate the ultimate pessimism of the film becomes more marked as the narrative progresses towards Frady's failure and death. There is a contrast between the process of investigation and the composition of shots in the last section of the film. As Frady uncovers more clues and seems to be getting closer to the truth behind the conspiracy he is shown to be increasingly insignificant

2 This emphasis on the idea of seeing and not seeing is central to *Hidden* (Haneke, 2005)(see Chapter 3).

in the mise en scène. The mise en scène emphasises the man-made, designed aspect of the environment, which is in contrast to the natural beauty of the mountains and pine trees of Salmon Tail, the small town Frady visits at the beginning of the investigation. In the city, buildings tower over him, the perspective is exaggerated in interior locations to place Frady as a tiny figure, a metaphor for his inability to change anything.

In contrast to the wide-open spaces which connote fear and suspicion, low-key lighting and a traditional mise en scène is often used to signify trust and safety. The office of Frady's news-editor and friend and the bar in Salmon Tail share a similar style which refers to history and roots. 'Happy hour' in Salmon Tail at first seems threatening, despite the beauty of the mountain setting. The bar signifies the opposition between city and the country. The customers are dressed in cowboy-influenced fashions, the bar is oak-panelled and rustic with gingham-checked tablecloths and wagon wheels hanging from the ceiling. The women are 'hostesses', clearly there for decoration and pleasure. Frady is initially regarded with suspicion, suggesting a hostile, dangerous place but it is soon apparent that the inhabitants of Salmon Tail are trustworthy, down to earth and open, unlike the people of the city. As Lev (2000: 53) points out, though, darkness is also used more conventionally in the climactic scenes above the convention centre on the dark, anonymous walkways: 'There is no personality, no history to the catwalks and corridors . . . and this makes them an apt setting for an assassination without apparent roots or motives'. This use of the darkness which hides the guilty and creates anonymity is also evident in the scenes of the government commission at the beginning and end of the film, where the 'official version' is handed down.

A more marked judgement on contemporary society is created through the opposition between the small town and city culture in *Klute*, with John Klute and Bree symbolising opposing sides of the divide. The connotations of these oppositions are to do with criminal and non-criminal behaviour but within that context is a comment on acceptable gender roles. As the 'city girl', Bree has been corrupted: the 1970s feminist symbol of the working woman is here linked to prostitution with Bree making money from selling sex and from her appearance (as a model and actress). The ending of the film rescues Bree from the city, taking her to the safety and traditional gender roles of the small town. The city represents a disruption to the apparently natural expression of femininity and masculinity revealing these to be an ideological construction; when Frady goes to Salmon Tail he is addressed as 'Miss' because of his long hair, the fact that he orders a non-alcoholic drink and shows no sexual interest in the female staff.

The representation of the opposition between the city and the country (or unnatural and natural worlds) in the political crime thriller draws together ideological concerns which are repeatedly explored in the crime genre – the contemporary anxiety about gender roles which here find their expression in the 'fragmented, postmodern man' (Lev, 2000: 52). The heroes of these films are characterised by their lack of roots or family ties, they are typical of the hero role in that they never reach a stable equilibrium but are instead always in *media res*. The lack of family in the conspiracy thriller is part of the films' comment on America in the early 1970s and another way in which the films can be read as a conservative form. There is in the films a sense that something had gone wrong at the level of nation and therefore also in the structure that symbolises the working of society at a micro-level – the family. Alan J. Pakula, the director of *The Parallax View*, makes specific reference to this when discussing the character of the newspaper editor and the mise en scène of his office:

> It represented a family, a man who was rooted, a whole American tradition that was dying, an anachronism, as compared to this totally cold and enormously bizarre world that Beatty goes after, and in comparison to his own character, which is the totally rootless modern man.

> (in Lev, 2000: 53)

The use of the family, or lack of it, to make an ideological point is particularly evident when the crime film is combined with the melodrama. The hybrid form provides a context for the crime film to explore the workings of the family in a more cynical manner than in much classical Hollywood cinema.

THE CRIME FAMILY

The family in the crime film is usually synonymous with the 'crime family' of the gangster film which foregrounds the family at the level of plot (warfare between the 'families') and ideology (the importance of family values). The reading of the family in the gangster film has been influenced by theories on the function of melodrama, specifically that the family represents the capitalist society with all its constraints and contradictions.

The Godfather films are characteristic of the gangster film in their representation of the family. The importance of family is continually reinforced – belonging to the Corleones by blood is a form of sacrament. The set pieces reflect this with the trilogy structured around family celebrations such as weddings and christenings. On the day of his daughter's wedding the godfather must grant any request brought to him, signifying the almost magical quality of the family event. This familial focus is also typical of the stereotypes which the gangster films use to represent Italian Americans. The emphasis on the important events of family life, which are more commonly associated with female genres, are one of the elements of the gangster film which overlaps with melodrama. It is the melodrama which foregrounds areas more usually seen as domestic and secondary to the external, active world of the male. The crime film shares with the melodrama a complex analysis of the function of the family; this reading of the gangster film is based on the Marxist understanding of the family's role in society.

This position sees the way that the family is privileged in capitalist society as ideological. The family provides an outlet for the worker to fulfil 'his' desire for achievement without disrupting the class hierarchy; this focus on the family also has the benefit for capitalism of producing the next generation of the workforce. The family unit is a microcosm of the capitalist system as it is also a hierarchical structure with the patriarch at the top able to give orders to his wife and children and have them submit to him. There are threats to this miniature model of capitalism though: the father may not be up to the task of running the family and training his son to take his place; the position of the woman as passive in the family is problematic and might cause disruption to the hierarchy. The claustrophobic nature of the family which comes from self-reliance can also lead to unnatural sexual relationships which will ultimately destroy it. It is this paradox inherent in the family, that it can be destroyed from within, which drives the narrative of the gangster film: 'From such a perspective, the gangster's characteristic obsession with preserving his family, which nonetheless leads ineluctably to its destruction, is immensely revealing' (Langford, 2005: 141). Langford traces this narrative back to the classic gangster films of the 1930s. In *Scarface*, Tony Camonte's drive for success is in parallel to the doomed incestuous relationship with his sister.

In *The Godfather* Part I and II, Michael Corleone is never able to equal the success of his father Vito as the head of the family; it is an Oedipal drama where the son's failure leads to the destruction of the family. Michael's narrative progression to achieve wealth and power for the family (rather than for himself) is mirrored in the simultaneous destruction of the family he supposedly wants to protect. This narrative route is defined by Michael's murder of his brother Fredo but also includes the murder of his brother-in-law and his indirect responsibility for the death of his daughter (*Godfather III*). The murder of Fredo is particularly indicative of the contradictions of the crime film family. Michael orders that 'nothing must happen to Fredo' while his mother is alive, but that when she dies he will be killed. The primacy of the family ends with the previous generation and Michael's ruthlessness is victorious: 'Michael's blind pursuit of power, ostensibly in the name of the family, unleashes uncontainable forces that must ultimately destroy it' (Langford, 2005: 142). In this reading the crime family in the gangster film is a symbol for capitalism, while the inevitable destruction of the family is a comment on the inequities of the system which is in conflict with the qualities needed to nurture family values. In *The Godfather* the criminal activities of the gangster reflect the corruption of the state, much in the same way that the conspiracy thrillers do: the individual is symbolic of the social. In melodrama the focus is much more on the effect on the individual, specifically the female, under capitalism.

CRIME AND THE MELODRAMA

The exploration of the role and meaning of the family in film has been particularly focused on the study of melodrama. The intersection of the crime genre with melodrama explores the effect of violence in the domestic rather than the public sphere. The subject of the alienation within the family and wider society is played out against the competing forms of melodrama and the crime film. The following section examines the way in which this hybrid form has been analysed, with particular reference to feminist approaches.

In the 1930s and 1940s, films which are now defined as gangster and film noir were routinely referred to dismissively as melodrama by the industry and critics (see Neale, 1999). This highlights the pejorative use of the term, which alluded to melodrama's emphasis on the compression of a series of dramatic events, coincidences, sudden reversals and reliance on emotional response from the audience. Overall the term characterised the perceived lack of realism in the form. Within film studies a definition of melodrama was developed by feminist critics in the 1980s to focus on gender and social roles. In this definition melodrama was characterised in terms of sexual difference, those with a male central character and those with a female. The masculine and feminine form of the genre performed different functions with the former focusing on reconciliation and equilibrium; the latter on unfulfilled desires (see Mulvey, 1987). A criminal act is frequently the focus of the melodrama, contributing to the moral dilemma which is central to the form. The crime tends to be driven by emotion and individual psychology; in contrast to the crime film it does not focus on the investigation by agents of the state but remains within the 'family'. The dramatic knot of the melodrama narrative, where different storylines and characters are threaded together, is similar to the way in which the strands of an investigation are pursued in the detective film, allowing the two forms to intersect.

This similarity and difference in form between crime and melodrama is most explicitly analysed in feminist approaches to film noir: 'as a genre it [melodrama] remains remarkably unfixed in that traces of its generic make up can be found in many other genres or subgenres (such as the thriller – especially the film noir)' (Hayward 2002: 218). The following considers the ideological position of the crime melodrama hybrid in masculine and feminine examples of the genre.

Film noir and the family

In 'Woman's Place: The Absent Family of Film Noir' (1989: 23), Harvey encapsulates the effect on the representation of the family when the crime film (in this case, film noir) and melodrama meet:

> It is the representation of the institution of the family, which in so many films serves as the mechanism whereby desire is fulfilled, or at least ideological equilibrium established, that in film noir serves as the vehicle for the expression of frustration.

The introduction of the crime form (which is different from a melodrama which includes a crime) makes explicit the themes of instability within the family. In many examples of the film-noir cycle of the 1940s and 1950s, the family and the domestic sphere is repeatedly represented as stifling and claustrophobic for women, a place to escape from rather than to find refuge in. In Double Indemnity (1944),

Walter Neff (Fred MacMurray), an insurance salesman, is seduced by a married woman, Phyllis Dietrichson (Barbara Stanwyck) and they plot to murder her husband. The lovers carry out the murder but ultimately kill each other. The story unfolds in flashback (a convention of both melodrama and film noir) and is told from the point of view of Walter, a perspective underlined by the use of voiceover. Harvey (1989) demonstrates how the film emphasises all the paradoxes and instability inherent in the family in capitalism. Here it is understandable that Phyllis would want to escape the family home where 'three people who hate each other spend endlessly boring evenings together' (1989: 29). Similarly, Walter's desire to escape the monotony of corporate life, represented in the mise en scène of the dark offices filled with regimented desks, is also explicable. The function of the melodramatic form is to smooth over these inherent contradictions and to reconcile the family at the end of the film. The disruption caused by the crime narrative of murder and investigation, however, makes this impossible. Walter and Phyllis are punished for their crime, but the crime against the family is so great – murder rather than unfaithfulness – that the narrative is unable to hide the cracks in the family, going so far as to provoke the idea of alternative forms to the institution: 'Despite the ritual punishment of acts of aggression, the vitality with which these are endowed produces an excess of meaning that cannot finally be contained' (Harvey, 1989: 33).

In 'Duplicity in Mildred Pierce' (1989), Cook argues that the melodrama and the crime film work antagonistically to each other, the one representing the feminine domestic sphere, the other the public masculine space: 'It seems that a basic split is created in the film between melodrama and film noir, between "Woman's film" and "Man's film", a split which indicates the presence of two voices, female and male' (1989: 71). The creation of two voices through this mix of forms has the effect of creating 'excess', as classical Hollywood narration is normally unified with one voice. The concept of excess in film theory suggests that sometimes elements such as the narrative, mise en scene or a star performance can be so stylised and exaggerated that it creates a different meaning to the obvious, surface one. *Mildred Pierce* (1945) is excessive in all these areas often due to the effect of mixing genres. These areas of excess include the performance of Joan Crawford, the narrative and use of genre. The narrative is packed full of melodramatic events such as a rags-to-riches story, marital break-up, love affairs, mother–daughter relationships, as well as the murder and investigation of film noir. The mise en scène is excessive both due to the characteristic styles of film noir and melodrama and the effect of the contrast between them. In Cook's analysis the excess, which is symbolic of the woman's escape from patriarchy (Mildred rejects her husband and sets up a successful restaurant business), has to be controlled by the narrative. This is the ideological function of the film-noir crime narrative and the role of the detective.

Mildred Pierce is structured in flashbacks told from Mildred's point of view. The difference from films such as *Double Indemnity* is, as Cook points out, the duplicity associated with Mildred, which encourages the audience to distrust her. Mildred has confessed to the murder of her second husband to protect her daughter who is the murderer. This information is kept from the audience until the end of the film when the detective reveals that he knew Mildred was lying throughout, effectively undermining her story and voice. For Cook, the detective signifies the Law and Patriarchy; he is in the role of confessor to Mildred. Mildred's crime is not murder, but her betrayal of the family and her attempt to take the place of the father. It is this transgression which has led to murder. The formal structure of the film reinforces this. The melodrama form, when Mildred was independent and successful, are in the past, told in flashback. The crime film of the present focuses on Mildred's duplicity, emphasised by the low-key lighting which casts shadows across her face, the murder itself and the setting of the police station. The ultimate dominance of the 'male voice' in *Mildred Pierce* is, Cook argues, apparent in the final image of the film. Here Mildred is led away from the police station by her first husband, Bert, the mise en scène emphasising the monumental, dominating, architecture of the police station and the female cleaners scrubbing the steps.

Mildred's downfall – which includes the death of her youngest daughter, the separation from her older daughter Veda, and the destruction of her business – is the consequence of her obsessive devotion to her daughter: 'Veda is part of me', she states. The film suggests that this refusal to let go of her daughter is unnatural and leads inexorably to the crime of murder. In this narrative paradox, where Mildred destroys the very thing that her actions were intended to save, the film noir/melodrama repeats a similar pattern to the gangster film's destruction of the family. This ambiguity in film noir, where the family is both destroyed and rescued by the narrative, is typical of the female melodrama where female desire cannot be expressed because it will lead to chaos. The crime melodrama *Mystic River* (Eastwood, 2003) can be defined as a hybrid male melodrama and police procedural; it deals with the crime genre themes of revenge and retribution in the context of the melodramatic family.

THE CRIME/MELODRAMA HYBRID

Mystic River has been controversial due to its depiction of revenge and the representation of gender relationships within the family. Rosenbaum (2003) reads the themes of the film as working to validate a need for vengeance which could be applied to wider social and cultural contexts:

> A desire for revenge – no matter how illogical, misguided, and ultimately disastrous its premises might be – is probably the most validated emotion in current American movies and current American politics. It's seen as so noble and righteous that for some it justifies a loss of civil liberties, as well as capital punishment, holy wars, and collateral damage. Even if the wrong people die, at least we know our intentions were good. This is a form of popular psychosis.

Placing the film in the context of the crime/melodrama hybrid suggests a more ambiguous meaning in the reading of the representations of the family and society.

Mystic River focuses on three male characters – Jimmy (Sean Penn), Dave (Tim Robbins) and Sean (Kevin Bacon) – who were childhood friends but have grown apart. It is structured around five crimes, four of which are murders. The narrative twists, coincidences and revelations of the crime investigation demonstrate the influence of melodrama. The film is set in South Boston and opens in flashback when the first crime takes place: as a child Dave was abducted and abused by paedophiles who were never caught. As adults the three have been estranged but their lives become connected again when Jimmy's daughter, Katie, is murdered and Sean, now a police detective, investigates the crime. In the course of the investigation it is also revealed that Jimmy had killed a man in the past, Ray Harris, who had informed on him, sending him to prison for three years. Ray's son is Katie's killer. In the present, Dave murders a suspected paedophile in revenge for the crime committed against him. The

Figure 4.4 Mystic River: the collision of police procedural and male melodrama

final murder is committed when Jimmy kills Dave, wrongly believing him to be his daughter's murderer. The narration is restricted in the manner of a 'whodunit', the audience find out the identity of the murderers as the police do.

The structure of Mystic River can be compared to Mildred Pierce in the way in which the two forms – police procedural and male melodrama – intertwine. In this sense there are also two voices, both male, both authoratative. The conventions of melodrama are clear from the start. The three boys are playing hockey in the street when a car pulls up and the driver makes Dave get in the car. This introduces several conventions of melodrama. These include the small-town setting of the Boston suburbs which are signified as a local community where everyone knows everyone else. In melodrama there is often a dominating event from the past, in this case Dave's abduction, which will affect the present and future. The narrative of melodrama is shaped by the effect of chance and coincidence: how might Sean and Jimmy's lives have changed if they had also got in the car?

The melodramatic sphere of the film includes the mise en scène of the triple decker homes, decorated inside with paintings and family photos, the washing hanging over the balconies. The sense of a small town is intensified by people's proximity to each other: they walk the streets and shop at the local store owned by Jimmy, the quaintly named 'Cottage Market'. Only Katie, who is murdered, and the detectives investigating the murder are shown driving. Celeste, Dave's wife, refers to being in her car, but only as a place to sit and think. The static nature of small-town family life is what Katie is desperate to get away from. On the day she is murdered she is intending to escape to Las Vegas with her boyfriend, Brendan. Within the closeness of the community it is possible to be simultaneously distanced and alienated: Dave says that he's known Jimmy's daughter Katie all his life but he hasn't been friends with Jimmy since his abduction.

The domestic space of Mystic River is a place of conflict and misery, often signified by the deviation from the nuclear 'norm'.

All the families have been disrupted in some way, creating an unstable situation: Jimmy's first wife and the mother of Katie died while he was in prison for robbery; Sean's wife has left him and taken their baby girl; Brendan's mother is a bitter, angry woman after her husband (apparently) abandoned her. All family life is riven with tension: Jimmy's angry exchanges with his father-in-law at Katie's wake; his wife's unhappiness at his favouritism of Katie over their other daughters (Jimmy's relationship with Katie is signified as being too close, in some way unnatural). The desperate nature of family life in Mystic River seems too great to be resolved by the narrative.

The crime committed against Dave is the event from the past which shapes the present, a characteristic of melodrama. The film examines the way in which the victim can become blamed for their own situation; they are an unpleasant reminder of something terrible which could threaten the safety of the family and community. 'Damged goods' is the verdict on Dave when he returns home after the abduction. Despite his position as husband and father he is only ever seen as marginal in contrast to the masculine heroes, Sean and Jimmy, and he is unable to take up his position as patriarch.

The five crimes which are part of the film's narration are all violent, terrible crimes against individuals. Three of the murders – Jimmy's murders of Ray Harris and Dave, Dave's murder of a paedophile – are motivated by retribution. The crime against Dave as a child and the murder of Katie, which becomes the focus for the investigation of the film, are seemingly random, inexplicable events which are given meaning and motivation by the structure of the narration. With the exception of the crime that takes place in childhood, the identities of the criminals are withheld from the audience until the final, climactic sequences. This creates an emotional alignment with characters and effects of suspense and horror. The restricted narration also provides the spectator with the pleasures of enigma and resolution.

Two types of justice

The police procedural, detective aspect of *Mystic River* uses many of the expected conventions of the form. A 'buddy' pair leads the investigation: Sean, an Irish American who grew up with the people now under investigation, and Whitey Powers (Laurence Fishburne), an African American who is an outsider. In all the shots of the community, there is no evidence of a racial mix, emphasising the closed nature of the setting. The character of Sean is a classic detective figure. The people from his old neighborhood treat him with suspicion, but neither does he fit comfortably with his police colleagues. Sean's marginalised position is underlined by the break-up of his marriage: he is a husband and father without a wife and child. Whitey is concerned that Sean will allow his connection to his old community to affect his judgment in the investigation and although Sean denies this, it is exactly what happens. By the end of the film, Sean has accepted Jimmy's brand of vigilante justice over the workings of the judicial system.

The murder of Jimmy's daughter is the catalyst for the crime narrative and the focus of the investigation. From the outset, the police are separate from, even in conflict with, the community. When Katie's body is discovered, her father is held back from the crime scene, an action that provokes anger and violence between Jimmy's friends and the police. The raw emotion of the scene emphasises Jimmy's loss but also sets up two factions, both determined to find the murderer and bring him to justice, but through different methods. Jimmy and Sean are the figureheads of each operation, representing charismatic and legal justice. As the investigation progresses, the police are frustrated by the unofficial investigation carried out by Jimmy and his supporters, the Savage brothers, who cajole and frighten witnesses. Jimmy's orchestration of the investigation positions him in opposition but equal to Sean. The iconography of Jimmy's gang suggests the gangster film, black leather jackets, gold jewellery, shades, cigars, beer and whisky, but without any organised crime to oversee it becomes a personal fiefdom; Jimmy is the patriarch of South Boston.

The official police investigation is structured conventionally, developed through a series of witness interviews, forensic analysis and intuition. The investigation reveals layers of connection to Katie's murder across the community that leads back into the past. The detectives solve Katie's murder through attention to detail and deduction: they hear something unusual on a 911 recording which leads them to the realisation that two young men, Ray Harris Jr and his friend Sean are the killers. The solution to the crime is revealed simultaneously to the detectives and the audience at this stage but for the remainder of the film the audience is in a superior position as the events are told in omniscient narration.

The murder of Katie is described as an accident, something that the murderers did not intend to happen, but the organisation of events provides motive and inevitability to the crime. This suggests that the attitude to revenge and vigilante justice in Mystic River is ambiguous. The murder of Katie, the terrible thing that nearly destroys Jimmy, is random and motiveless at the level of plot. The film's narration does, though, provide a reason for her death. Katie's killer is the son of Ray Harris. As Jimmy confesses to the killing of Ray Harris before murdering Dave, the film cuts to Brendan and Ray Jr, linking their actions to those of Jimmy's in the past. The murder of Katie, whether intentional or not, provides Ray with revenge for the death of his father. The organisation of the events suggests the inevitability of tragedy coming from vigilante justice. The narration also places the audience in a position of shock and helplessness as the revelations are made, affecting the spectator response to the actions of the characters, particularly Jimmy's.

The two types of justice, legal and charismatic, are played out in the climactic sequence of revelation at the end of the film. The sequence is organised through cross-cutting, which moves between three locations, giving the spectator access to more information than any of the individual characters have. The dominant part of the sequence takes place in a run-down bar on the banks of the Mystic River where Dave is interrogated by Jimmy and the Savage brothers.

The sequence cross-cuts between this, the police station where Sean and Whitey discover the identity of Katie's killer, and Brendan's flat where he accuses his brother of Katie's murder. The mise en scène of the sequence reiterates the similarities and differences between Sean and Jimmy. Sean's desk at the police station is piled with evidence and points to his position in the rational, judicial system. The setting of the run-down, isolated bar and the presence of his criminal henchman position Jimmy as an outlaw, dispensing retribution.

In a similar way to Mildred in *Mildred Pierce*, Dave is set up as a suspect and constructed as duplicitous. The audience is encouraged to view Dave as guilty of Katie's murder. On the night of her death, he is shown watching her dance provocatively in a bar and he comes home late, covered in cuts and blood. His story that he was in a fight with a mugger does not convince his wife or the audience. The audience's emotional response to Dave is manipulated in order to find him less appealing than the more active, dominant characters of Sean and Jimmy. Dave is a tormented figure, the violence done to him in the past, the melodrama reading suggests, prevents him from taking up his position in patriarchy. Rather than representing him sympathetically, he is placed repeatedly in a dark mise en scène or shot from behind as he shambles along the street. At times, he is menacing and threatening, sat in the dark, 'thinking about vampires', drinking too much. Dave's tortured aspect suggests that he is guilty and must pose a continual threat to the neighbourhood, even to his own family. The negative emotional reaction to his character is underlined by Tim Robbins's performance. Through this, Dave becomes a shuffling, diffident presence – with his stooped posture and head down he is uncomfortable in his height rather than proud of his ability to dominate the people around him. The ultimate suspicion that Dave really is 'damaged goods' comes when Celeste confesses her suspicions to Jimmy, betraying her husband and sealing his fate.

Dave is a passive figure, signified as feminine and therefore 'unnatural' in the traditional family. Celeste is the active partner, working to support the family, helping their friends in mourning, investigating

Dave's alibi. In the melodrama, Dave functions as a symbol of excess and therefore has to be removed. He is a reminder that the family can be broken and disrupted, that it is a site of repression and alienation. In the context of the melodrama, Dave is guilty because he has not been able to take up his correct position as a dominant husband and father. This narrative framework, where Jimmy 'gets' Dave and Sean 'gets' the killers of Katie, has a perfect logic and seems to reveal the viewpoint of the film: Jimmy is protecting the family and Dave symbolises a threat to that, even though he is innocent of Katie's murder. The closing sequence of the film, however, which takes place in the aftermath of the criminal events, subverts this initial ideological reading.

The final shots of the film reinstate the supremacy of the family in the community. The setting is a traditional neighbourhood parade with floats, marching bands and majorettes. Sean has been reunited with his estranged wife and baby and they now stand close together, he with a protective arm around her shoulders. Across the street, Jimmy's wife stands with her daughters, surrounded by her husband's supporters, soon to be joined by Jimmy. They are an impregnable force, a barrier constructed for safety and security that keeps out anyone who might threaten it. Sean exchanges a mock salute, his hand forming a gun, with Jimmy, the murderer, small-time gangster and patriarch. This recognition between the two men in which the police detective acknowledges the right of the agent of charismatic law to carry out his own justice has been read as an apologia for individual vigilantism or, in a wider context, for a nation's response to attack. The sinister representation of the family with its gangster bodyguards and lack of pity for Celeste as she searches for her lost husband suggests, at the least, that this form of justice comes at a very high price.[3] Ultimately, *Mystic River* represents an isolated, claustrophobic community that seems an

3 The film can also be read in the context of its director, Clint Eastwood's later films. These constitute a revision of some of the myths and ideologies constructed by his iconic detective and cowboy roles. *Mystic River*, along with *Unforgiven* and *Gran Torino*, is a repudiation of vigilante behaviour, questioning the cost of such actions.

anachronism of traditional values. Masculinity and femininity are as clearly delineated as in the film noirs of the 1940s and a return to charismatic law inevitably ends in tragedy. The extreme actions of vigilante justice and murder, which are needed to maintain the dominance of the family, are too great to be recouped by the narrative.

The political crime films of the 1970s and film noir in the 1940s are two periods of the genre which have become cultural touchstones, resonating with audiences at the time and continuing to exert a thematic and stylistic influence in film. The figure of the femme fatale personified an anxiety in society about changing gender roles and the effect of this on the family. The failed hero of the 1970s crime thriller functions as a symbol for despair and pessimism. In both cases, the story of the crime provides a framework to comment on these themes: the state committing crime against the powerless individual; the individual attacking the family and by implication the foundation of capitalist society. In all the examples discussed in this chapter, the resolution of the story of the crime fails to provide reassurance for the audience as is conventional in classic narrative. When the guilty are punished, their excess has already been too great to be recouped by the new equilibrium, suggesting that, in the case of film noir, the future of the nuclear family is uncertain. The more ambiguous unresolved endings of the political crime film reflect a new realism of the period in which a lone hero cannot counter the corrupt workings of society. In the political crime films the judicial system is absent, part of the conspiracy of the state which can no longer be trusted. The common theme of conflict of the crime genre, the choice between state-sanctioned justice and retribution carried out by an individual, is no longer relevant. This is central to the unsettling nature of these films: the certainties held by each side of that opposition has disappeared, the hero does not know whom he is chasing or what crimes have been committed, it is no longer a personal or moral crusade. The intersection of the contemporary melodrama and crime film in *Mystic River* plays out this ongoing theme of the crime film, the question of justice. It is a return to a more conservative world view in the sense that there is still a choice between the law and the vigilante, but the film is clear on the cost to the family, community and society of choosing vigilante justice.

The influence of the political crime films is evident in contemporary crime films where conspiracy has become a conventional part of the representation of big business and government: *Enemy of the State*(1998) crosses the conspiracy crime film with the Hitchcock thriller in the plot of a man on the run due to mistaken identity; *Michael Clayton* (2007) and *The Constant Gardener* focus on the corruption in corporations (chemicals and pharmaceuticals respectively). The action thriller hybrid, *The Bourne Identity* (2002) and its sequels, employs several of the themes of the 1970s films. Jason Bourne is a man without a memory or identity, and the government that he worked for, as a CIA agent, is now trying to kill him. Like his 1970s predecessors, he is *in media res*, unable to reach a resolution. In great contrast to the earlier films, Bourne is an action hero and trained assassin able to defeat his opponents.

ONGOING INVESTIGATIONS

The hybrid nature – and commercial success – of the *Bourne* films is characteristic of a new style of crime film, the crime/action/sci-fi hybrid such as *Inception* (2010) and *Source Code* (2011) (*Minority Report* (2002) can be read as a precursor to these films). This new trend in the crime genre is conventional in its use of a hero who is investigating an enigma, but the focus is more on a psychological investigation into the distinction between reality and illusion – if indeed the two concepts can be separated. Instead of taking place against the backdrop of a recognisable society with its actual problems and conflicts, the story unfolds in a manufactured reality, closer to a dream, removing some of the possibility of political and cultural commentary usually associated with the crime film. The films take place in a manufactured reality using the grammar of video games – the repetitions, narrative levels and goals that the hero has to encounter – to reinforce the theme of a parallel reality. The thematic concerns explore contemporary anxieties such as the effect of new technology and the development of cyberspace. With their fractured and ambiguous narratives, which are a major part of their appeal, the investigator is once again lost in a world he (and the hero is still usually a man) no longer understands and has to learn new rules to survive. This is also a central characteristic of *Shutter Island*, in which the FBI agent (Leonardo DiCaprio) is unwittingly investigating his own crime.

The history of the crime film has encompassed a wide range of styles and characters. This includes the expressionism of film noir, the formal experimentation of the 1970s, the tragic figure of the gangster, the maverick detective and action heroes. The thematic preoccupations have remained constant: the exploration of the border between the criminal and non-criminal. The shifting nature of this border represents the changing norms of society at different periods, and who is judged to be within and without mainstream society. This focus has developed to engage with wider philosophical questions of identity and existence. The investigative structure has become a means to express the attempt by individuals to create order from chaos, to give meaning to events that are incomprehensible.

The recent hybrid crime film with its high concept, big budget and special effects exists alongside more traditional examples of the genre, where the pleasures of the story of the crime and its investigation retain a familiar appeal. *The Girl with the Dragon Tattoo*, while sharing some of the same concerns about the virtual world as *Inception*, is a narrative in the tradition of the classic detective story with its enclosed community and cerebral, maverick detective. Similarly, *The Lincoln Lawyer* focuses on the investigation of crime and cover-up in the real world while also paying homage to the hardboiled detective films of the 1940s. Here, the central character, a criminal lawyer, is set up by a client who lies to him about his innocence. In the process of the attempt to clear his name, the film explores several of the structuring themes of the crime film: the inviolability of the law but the temptation to break it; the criminal justice system with its arcane processes as an essential barrier between good and evil; the attempt to explain the inexplicable through the structure of an investigation.

The crime film has a unique relationship with the audience, continually demanding an examination of the spectator's response to their alignment with anti-heroes and gangsters, the appeal of vigilantism and the pleasure of violence. One of the most enduring themes of the crime film is the negotiation of justice and retribution, dramatising the immediate satisfaction of the latter in the context of a moral dilemma. In this way, the crime film is continually able to comment on its contemporary social and political context, using the crime narrative to address a culture's most acute anxieties.

FILMOGRAPHY

2 Days in the Valley (John Herzfield, 1996, USA)
48 Hours (Walter Hill, 1982, USA)
All the President's Men (Alan J. Pakula, 1976, USA)
Angels with Dirty Faces (Michael Curtiz, 1937, USA)
Arlington Road (Mark Pellington, 1999, USA)
The Big Sleep (Howard Hawks, 1946, USA)
Bonnie and Clyde (Arthur Penn, 1968, USA)
The Bourne Identity (Doug Liman, 2002, USA)
Boys n the Hood (John Singleton, 1991, USA)
The Brave One (Neil Jordan, 2007, USA)
Breathless (Jean-Luc Godard, 1959, France)
Bullets or Ballots (William Keighly, 1936, USA)
The China Syndrome (James Bridges, 1979, USA)
Chinatown (Roman Polanski, 1974, USA)
Coma (Michael Crichton, 1978, USA)
The Conversation (Francis Ford Coppola, 1974, USA)
Coogan's Bluff (Don Siegal , 1968, USA)
Copycat (John Amiel, 1995, USA)
Crime School (Brian Foy, 1938, USA)
The Da Vinci Code (Ron Howard, 2006, USA)
Dead Presidents (Albert and Allen Hughes, 1995)

Death Wish (Michael Winner, 1974, USA)

Detour (Edgar G. Ulmer, 1945, USA)

Dirty Harry (Don Siegel, 1971, USA)

Disturbia (D.J. Caruso, 2007, USA)

Double Indemnity (Billy Wilder, 1944, USA)

Easy Rider (Dennis Hopper, 1969, USA)

Enemy of the State (Tony Scott, 1998, USA)

The Enforcer (James Fargo, 1976, USA)

Fargo (Joel Coen, 1996, USA)

Force of Evil (Abraham Polonsky, 1948, USA)

The Fugitive (Andrew Davis, 1993, USA)

G-Men (William Keighly, 1935, USA)

The Game (David Fincher, 1997, USA)

Get Carter (Mike Hodges, 1971, UK)

The Girl Who Played with Fire (Daniel Alfredson, 2009, Sweden)

The Girl Who Kicked the Hornet's Nest (Daniel Alfredson, 2009, Sweden)

The Girl with the Dragon Tattoo (Oplev, 2009, Sweden)

The Godfather (Francis Ford Copolla, 1972, USA)

The Godfather Part II (Francis Ford Copolla, 1974, USA)

The Godfather Part III (Francis Ford Copolla, 1990, USA)

Gone Baby Gone (Ben Affleck, 2007, USA)

Goodfellas (Martin Scorsese, 1991, USA)

Grosse Point Blank (George Armitage, 1997, USA)

La Haine (Mathieu Kassovitz, 1995, France)

Henry: Portrait of a Serial Killer (John McNaughton, 1986, USA)

Hidden (Michael Haneke, 2005, France)

The Ideas of March (D. Clooney, 2001)

Inception (Christopher Nolan, 2010, USA)

Kiss Me Deadly (Robert Aldrich, 1955, USA)

Klute (Alan J. Pakula, 1971, USA)

Leon (Luc Besson, 1994, France)

Lethal Weapon (Richard Donner, USA, 1987)

The Lincoln Lawyer (Brad Furman, 2011, USA)

Little Caesar (Mervyn LeRoy, 1930, USA)

Magnum Force (Ted Post, 1973, USA)

The Maltese Falcon (John Huston, 1941, USA)

Mean Streets (Martin Scorsese, 1973, USA)

Menace II Society (Albert and Allen Hughes, 1993, USA)

Michael Clayton (Tony Gilroy, 2007, USA)

Mildred Pierce (Michael Curtiz, 1945, USA)

Miller's Crossing (Ethan and Joel Cohn, 1990, USA)

Minority Report (Steven Spielberg, 2002, USA)

Missing (Costa-Gavras, 1982, USA)

Mystic River (Clint Eastwood, 2003, USA)

Natural Born Killers (Oliver Stone, 1994)

No Country for Old Men (Ethan and Joel Coen, 2007, USA)

North by Northwest (Alfred Hitchcock, 1959, USA)

Oldboy (Park Chan-wook, 2003, Korea)

Once Upon a Time in America (Sergio Leone, 1984, USA)

Out of the Past (Jacques Tourneur, 1947)

The Parallax View (Alan J. Pakula, 1974, USA)

Point Blank (John Boorman, 1967, USA)

Police, Adjective (Corneliu Purumboiu, 2009, Romania)

The Postman Always Rings Twice (Tay Garnet, 1946, USA)

Prince of the City (Sidney Lumet, 1981, USA)

The Public Enemy (William Wellman, 1931, USA)

Pulp Fiction (Quentin Tarantino, 1994, USA)

Rear Window (Alfred Hitchcock, 1954, USA)

Reservoir Dogs (Quentin Tarantino, 1992, USA)

The Roaring Twenties (Raoul Walsh, 1939, USA)

Romeo Is Bleeding (Peter Medak, 1993, USA)

Scarface (Howard Hawks, 1932, USA)

Scarface (Brian De Palma, 1983)

The Secret in Their Eyes (Juan Jose Campanella, 2009, Argentina)

Serpico (Sidney Lumet, 1981, USA)

Seven (David Fincher, 1995, USA)

Sexy Beast (Jonathan Grazer, 2000, USA)

Shadow of a Doubt (Alfred Hitchcock, 1943, USA)

Shutter Island (Martin Scorsese, 2010, USA)
The Silence of the Lambs (Jonathan Demme, 1991, USA)
Snatch (Guy Ritchie, 2000, UK)
Source Code (Duncan Jones, 2011, USA)
Sudden Impact (Clint Eastwood, 1983)
The Thin Man (W.S. Van Dyke, 1934)
Three Days of the Condor (Sydney Pollack, 1975, USA)
Walking Tall (Karlson, 1973, USA)
The Woman in the Window (Fritz Lang, 1944, USA)
Z (Costa-Gavras, 1969, France)
Zodiac (David Fincher, 2007, USA)

BIBLIOGRAPHY

Adorno, T. with Horkheimer, Max (2002 [1944]). 'The Culture Industry: Enlightenment as Mass Deception'. In *Dialectic of Enlightenment* (*Cultural Memory in the Present*). New York: Jephcott.

Alloway, L. (1971). *Violent America: the Movies 1946–64*. New York: MOMA.

Benjamin, W. (1992 [1929]) 'The Image of Proust' in *Illuminations*, London: Fontana Press.

Benjamin, W. (1992 [1936]) 'The Work of Art in the Age of Mechanical Reproduction'. In *Illuminations*. London: Fontana Press.

Biskind, P. (1998). *Easy Riders, Raging Bulls*. London: Bloomsbury.

Bordwell, D. (1989). *Making Meaning: Inference and Rhetoric in the Interpretation of Cinema*. Cambridge, MA: Harvard University Press.

Bordwell, D. (2007). *Poetics of Cinema*. London: Routledge.

Bordwell, D., Staiger, J. and Thompson, K. (1985). *The Classical Hollywood Cinema*. London: Routledge

Buscombe, E. (1970). 'The Idea of Genre in the American Cinema'. *Screen* 11/2, 33–45.

Cherry, B. (2009). *Horror*. London: Routledge

Clarens, C. (1980). *Crime Movies*. London: Secker and Warburg.

Clarkson, W. (1995). *Quentin Tarantino: Shooting from the Hip*. New York: Overlook Press.

Cook, P. (1989). 'Duplicity in Mildred Pierce'. In E. A. Kaplan, *Women in Film Noir* (pp. 68–82). London: BFI.

Dargis, M. (2005, March 25). 'The Violence (and the Seafood) is More than Raw'. Retrieved 25 April 2011, from *The New York Times*: http://movies.nytimes.com/2005/03/25/movies/25boy.html?_r=1

Davis, B. (1973). *The Thriller*. London: Studio Vista.

Derry,C. (1988) The Suspense Thriller: Films in the Shadow of Alfred Hitchcock. Jefferson, NC: McFarland and Co.

Drabble, Margaret (1985). 'Detective Fiction'. In *The Oxford Companion to English Literature*, Oxford: Oxford University Press.

Dyer, R. (1997). 'Kill and Kill Again'. *Sight and Sound*, 7 (9), 14–17.

Ferman, J. (1999) quoted in 'Entertainment Censor Attacks Film Violence' http://news.bbc.co.uk/1/hi/entertainment/349612.stm

Gates, P. (2004). 'A Brief History of the Detective Film'. Retrieved December 30, 2010, from Crimeculture: http://www.crimeculture.com/Contents/detectivefilm.htm

Gledhill, C. (2000). 'Rethinking Genre', in C. Gledhill and L. Williams (eds), *Reinventing Film Studies*. London: Arnold.

Gormley, P. (2005). *The New Brutality Film: Race and Affect in Contemporary Hollywood Cinema*. Bristol: Intellect Books.

Graysmith, R. (1996). *Zodiac*. New York: Berkley Publishing Group.

Gronstad, A. (2008). 'As I Lay Dying: Violence and Subjectivity in Tarantino's Reservoir Dogs'. In A. Gronstad, *Transfigurations: Violence, Death and Masculinity in American Cinema* (pp. 155–171). Amsterdam: Amsterdam University Press.

Gunning, T. (1990). 'The Cinema of Attractions'. In T. Elsaesser (ed.), *Early Cinema: Space, Frame,Narrative*. London: BFI.

Harvey, S. (1989). 'Woman's Place: The Absent Family of Film Noir'. In E. Kaplan (ed.), *Women in Film Noir* (pp. 22–34). London: BFI.

Hayward, S. (2002). *Cinema Studies: The Key Concepts*. London: Routledge.

Hendrix, G. (2006). 'Vengeance Is Theirs'. *Sight and Sound*, February.

Hill, J. (1998). 'The Political Thriller Debate'. In P. C. John Hill (ed.), *The Oxford Guide to Film Studies* (pp. 114–116). Oxford: Oxford University Press.

Kinder, M. (2001). 'Violence American Style: The Narrative Orchestration of Violent Attractions'. In J. D. Slocum (ed.), *Violence and American Cinema* (pp. 63–100). New York and London: Routledge.

Kochberg, S. (1996). 'Cinema as Institution'. In J. Nelmes (ed.), *An Introduction to Film Studies* (pp. 14–58). London: Routledge.

Kolker, R. (1988). *A Cinema of Loneliness*. Oxford: Oxford University Press.

Kolker, R. P. (1983). *The Altering Eye, Contemporary International Cinema*. New York: Oxford University Press.

Lane, A. (1994) 'Pulp Fiction'. In *Nobody's Perfect*. London: Picador

Langford, B. (2005). *Film Genre: Hollywood and Beyond*. Edinburgh: Edinburgh University Press.

Langman, L. A. (1995). *Guide to American Crime Films of the Forties and Fifties*. Westport, CT: Greenwood Press.

Leitch, T. (2002). *Crime Films*. Cambridge: Cambridge University Press.

Lev, P. (2000). *American Films of the 1970s: Conflicting Visions*. Austin: University of Texas Press.

McArthur, C. (1972). *Underworld USA*. London: Secker and Warburg.

MacCabe, C. (1981 [1974]). 'Realism and the Cinema: Notes on Some Brechtian Theses'. In Bennett et al. (eds), 1981, *Popular Television and Film*. London: Open University/BFI.

MacDonald, D. (1963). *Against the American Grain*. London: Gollanz.

Maltby, R. (2001). *Hollywood Cinema*. Oxford: Blackwell.

Miller, L. (2009)'The Banality of Virtue' at http://www.salon.com/09/reviews/fargo1.html

Mulvey, L. (1987). 'Notes on Sirk and Melodrama' (updated). In C. Gledhill (ed.), *Home Is Where the Heart Is: Studies in Melodrama and Woman's Film*. London: BFI.

Neale, S. (1990). 'Questions of Genre', *Screen* 31(1) 45–66.

Neale, S. (1999a). 'Contemporary Crime and the Detective Film'. In C. A. Bernink, *The Cinema Book* (pp. 172–181). London: BFI.

Neale, S. (1999b). 'Melodrama and the Woman's Film'. In S. Neale, *Genre and Hollywood* (pp. 168–192). London: Routledge.

Osterweil, A. (2006). Caché. *Film Quarterly*, 59 (4).

Porter, D. (1981). *The Pursuit of Crime, Art and Ideology in Detective Fiction*. New Haven: Yale University Press.

Rosenbaum, J. (2003). 'Vengeance Is Theirs'. Retrieved April 29, 2011, from jonathanrosenbaum.com: http://www.jonathanrosenbaum.com/?p=6107

Rotha, P. (1930[1967]). *The Film Till Now*. London: Spring Books.

Rutherford, A. (2002, Feb 21). 'Cinema and Embodied Affect'. Retrieved Jan 6, 2011, from Senses of Cinema: http://www.sensesofcinema.com/2003/feature-articles/embodied_affect/

Ryall, T. (1979). *Teachers' Study Guide 2*. London: BFI.

Ryall, T. (1998). 'Genre and Hollywood'. In John Hill and Pamela Church Gibson (eds), *The Oxford Guide to Film Studies* (pp. 327–38). Oxford: Oxford University Press.

Schatz, T. (1993). 'The New Hollywood'. In H. R. Jim Collins (ed.), *Film Theory Goes to the Movies* (pp. 8–36). London: Routledge.

Scorsese, Martin (1995). 'A Personal Journey with Martin Scorsese through American Movies', a documentary d. Scorsese.

Seydor, P. (1995, October). Sam Peckinpah. *Sight and Sound*.

Shadoian, J. (1977). *Dreams and Dead Ends: The American Gangster/Crime Film*. Cambridge: MIT Press.

Shaviro, S. (1993). *The Cinematic Body*. Minneapolis: University of Minnesota Press.

Slocum, J. (2001). 'Introduction: Violence and American Cinema: Notes for an Investigation'. In *Violence and American Cinema*, London: Routledge.

Smith, M. (1995). *Engaging Characters: Fiction, Emotion, and the Cinema*. Oxford: Clarendon Press.

Spelman, E. (1990). *Inessential Woman*. Boston, MA: Beacon Press.

Summerscale, K. (2008). 'The Prince of Sleuths'. *The Guardian* (5 April).

Thompson, Kirsten Moana (2007). *Crime Films: Investigating the Scene*. London: Wallflower Paperback.

Thomson, D. (2002). *The New Biographical Dictionary of Film*. London: Little Brown.

Todorov, T. (2006 [1977]). 'Poetics of Prose'. In D. Hale (ed.), *The Novel: An Anthology of Criticism* (pp. 205–19). Oxford: Blackwell.

Wagner, N. (2010). 'Turning Back Time: Duration, Simultaneity and the Timeless in Fitzgerald's and Fincher's *Benjamin Button*'. Retrieved April 29, 2011, from http://digitalarchive.gsu.edu/english_theses/85

Warshow, R. (2002a [1948]). 'The Gangster as Tragic Hero'. In R. Warshow, *The Immediate Experience*. New York: Doubleday.

Warshow, R. (2002b [1954]). 'Movie Chronicle: the Westerner'. In R. Warshow, *The Immediate Experience* (p. 106). New York: Doubleday.

Wollen, P. (1972). 'Conclusion'. In P. Wollen, *Signs and Meaning in the Cinema* (pp. 155–74). London: Secker and Warburg.

Young, A. (2010). *The Scene of Violence: Cinema Crime Affect*. London: Routledge.

INDEX